Published in 2002 by Laurence King Publishing Ltd
71 Great Russell Street
London WC1B 3BP
Tel: + 44 20 7430 8850
Fax: + 44 20 7430 8880
e-mail: enquiries@laurenceking.co.uk
www.laurenceking.co.uk

A catalogue record for this book is available from
the British Library.

ISBN: 1 85669 283 3

Printed in Hong Kong

Design: Richard Llewellyn

Front cover (left to right): Habbo Hotel, Horses for
Courses, 3D Groove, Temple of Heaven.
Front flap: B&D Music Videos.
Back flap: Spacelounge.
Back cover (left to right): Design Assembly, Mearns
and Gill

LAURENCE KING

WEB 3D

Stuart Dredge

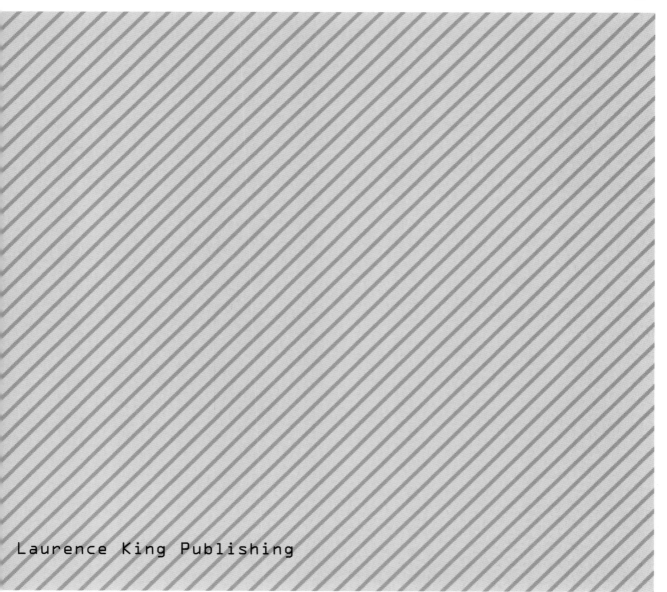

Laurence King Publishing

CONTENTS

INTRODUCTION

Web 3D has been the next big thing for more than five years now. Back then, it was hailed as the new revolution in a medium that was still in its infancy. It is no surprise that web designers had lofty ambitions — in the early years of the web, most sites followed the traditional print model of flat pages filled with text and pictures. Inspired by a heady mixture of virtual reality (VR) hype and sci-fi novels such as Neal Anderson's Snow Crash, many web designers were dreaming of a web full of immersive 3D worlds, with users — represented by virtual avatars — chatting, gaming, shopping or even holding business meetings in glorious 3D.

It seems far-fetched now, but here's a taste of those early ambitions. In February 1997, Gap announced that it was building a prototype online 3D store that would allow users to walk around a virtual Gap shop, pick up clothes and then buy them. Other retail chains were reportedly harbouring similar ambitions. Meanwhile, in March that year, Icelandic firm OZ Interactive signed a deal with Atlantic Records to build a VR concert arena online. Bands would play 'gigs' by slipping into motion-sensing body suits that would translate their movements to their avatars in the virtual arena, performing to crowds of equally virtual fans. This idea was actually taken seriously.

Later on that year, Ticketmaster announced that it would shortly be offering 3D seating previews and fly-bys on its website. This was perhaps a more sensible application for web 3D, but it was no more successful. It is these failures that have tarnished the reputation of online 3D as a workable concept ever since. Yet for anyone writing about web 3D now, it is essential to look back and assess the failures and successes — yes, there were some — of those early attempts.

VRML
Most of these attempts were based around Virtual Reality Modelling Language (VRML), a coding language used to create virtual environments and movement. As a specification, it was supposed to provide a standardized framework for the creation of 3D web content. Designers coded their own VRML worlds, or used authoring tools to create them, while users viewed the content in one of the various VRML browsers. The technology was hyped by its supporters and encouraged by a media looking for the next big thing. 'VRML is going to get into the hands of millions of users this year', promised Tony Parisi, Intervista president and co-author of the VRML standard, in January 1997. 'It's an acknowledgement that VRML technology kicks ass.'

By the end of that year, the only asses being kicked were those of designers still trying to sell their clients VRML content. Web 3D had failed to cross over into the mainstream for a variety of reasons that were summed up two years later by a rueful Parisi, speaking at the VRML 99 convention. He talked about the changes that would need to be made to VRML if you were to start from scratch. 'The browsers wouldn't be buggy, content written for one browser would work on another, there would be reasonable, human-readable programming interfaces and the plug-in download wouldn't be three goddamn megabytes,' he said, before adding a telling comment, 'What were we thinking?!'

VRML did flop, but that doesn't mean there wasn't any impressive content produced along the way. Silicon Graphics was one company that put its weight firmly behind VRML, and was responsible for commissioning some of the most innovative 3D content at the time — for example, Floops. This was a series of interactive animations, created by an agency called Protozoa, featuring a personable alien. Even today, its technical quality is still impressive.

VRML also saw limited success in the data-visualization market, particularly among scientists and government bodies. These niche — and usually offline — applications weren't enough to qualify it as a success. Despite their ambitious ideas, VRML developers never managed to persuade mainstream web users to come and check them out. In August 2001, posters to the comp.lang.vrml newsgroup discussed where VRML had gone wrong. 'There was great stuff showing up in little online contests,' remembered one person, 'but never anything of topical interest to the masses.'

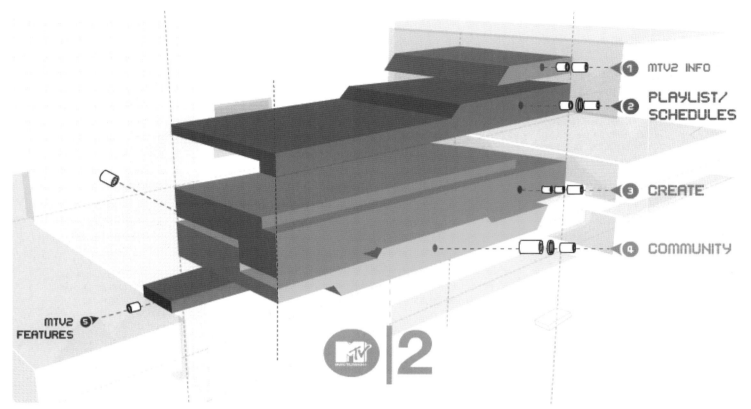

1 MTV2 INFO

2 PLAYLIST/ SCHEDULES

3 CREATE

4 COMMUNITY

MTV2 5 FEATURES

By 1998, the hype was over. Silicon Graphics had pulled out of the web 3D market, and VRML development had become the non-profit pursuit of a dwindling band of enthusiasts. In November, web usability guru Jakob Nielsen gleefully hammered what seemed like the final nail in its coffin in his online AlertBox column '2D is better than 3D'. Besides pointing out that both the screen and the mouse are 2D devices, Nielsen also highlighted the fact that most common interaction techniques — dragging, scrolling, etc. — are designed for 2D manipulation, thus leaving users confused when they have to deal with flying and zooming as well in a 3D world. Finally, he applied the coup de grace. 'The software needed for 3D is usually non-standard, crash-prone and requires an extra download (which users don't want to wait for).'

PARTIAL RECOVERY

VRML was seemingly dead in the water. However, designers were still exploring other ways of using 3D technologies online. Firms like the Groove Alliance and WildTangent were developing web game engines, for example, while others like Viewpoint, Cycore and Superscape were concentrating on visualization tools that could create 3D models for ecommerce websites. Meanwhile, firms such as Pulse and Digimask were working on avatar-based technologies to create animated 3D web characters. Finally, the concept of 3D chatworlds was being kept alive by the likes of ActiveWorlds and Worlds.com.

And then there was Boo.com. In 1999, two young Swedish entrepreneurs launched the largest dotcom yet. Ernst Malmsten and Kajsa Leander's plan was to sell sports and leisure clothing online, complete with 3D models of every product that users could spin around to view from every angle. It seemed like a great idea, but the technology was expensive and unwieldy.

Although by no means the only cause of Boo.com's downfall, the spinnable 3D products became an easy scapegoat in the media. When Boo folded in May 2000, the internal design team was working on a quicker, slicker 3D system that used dHTML rather than Flash for the site's relaunch. But it never went live. Boo.com convinced many businesses that web 3D and ecommerce weren't a good match — an assumption that still lingers today.

Despite this failure, many web designers hadn't lost their enthusiasm for 3D technologies, and they now had a new tool to play with. In June 1999, Macromedia launched Flash 4. Although still predominantly a 2D animation and site-building tool, its newly-introduced ActionScripting functionality enabled designers to add more complex interactivity to their Flash work. Many started to produce 3D Flash content, either using their own custom-built software alongside Flash, or third-party tools such as Swift 3D or Strata 3D. In June 2000, this culminated in the launch of MTV2 — a website created by the London agency Digit for MTV's alternative music channel. The site used a relatively simple 3D interface, but it garnered a huge buzz among the global web-design community — and inspired a stream of copycat sites.

MACROMEDIA

Even as creatives were discovering Flash's potential for 3D work, Macromedia was working on a new initiative of its own. In July 2000, the firm announced that it was working with Intel to implement 3D functionality in the next version of its Shockwave player. The deal involved 3D-graphics technology developed at Intel's Architecture Lab. 'Our joint development efforts with Intel will bring the realism and impact of interactive 3D to e-merchandising, e-learning and entertainment on the web', promised Diane Rogers,

□ NATIONAL GEOGRAPHIC
OUTPOST

CONGO TREK
A JOURNEY THROUGH THE HEART OF CENTRAL AFRICA

CONGO TREK 360° | DISPATCHES & MAP | CLASSROOM IDEAS | RESOURCES & LINKS | CREDITS

CONGO TREK 360

Explore the Congo River Basin—virtually. Move your mouse around the 360° image at left and click on animals and objects for videos, audio, and accounts of life in extreme Africa.

Explorer J. Michael Fay hiked 1,200 miles (2,000 kilometers) through central Africa to encounter the creatures in our image: gorillas, chimps, elephants, humans. Here you can experience them all in one spot—something you'd probably never be able to do in the wild.

Throughout the 15-month "Megatransect," Fay compiled data, video, and photos of largely untouched but threatened wilderness—all part of his epic effort to help understand and conserve the Congo Basin.

Related site: Online-only field notes, photos, and video from *National Geographic magazine's* coverage of the trek

[Note: Pop-up window must stay open in order to view Congo Trek 360. To open a new Pop-up window, reload this page.]

Photograph by Michael Nichols

01:30:16

X

Target Acquired :
Hotel Metropole
ETA: 01:31:37

SHADOWCAM | LEGOCAM | SNAPSHOT

COMMLINK

Heads up, Op, I've got a sharper at Hotel Metropole. A woman. Nailed 'em with a tracer so you should see a red X on your map. Get to it by 01:31:37 to pick up the trail.

COMMAND
SPYLOG
DOSSIERS
CASEBOOK
HELP

Macromedia's vice president of product management. In April 2001, Director 8.5 Shockwave Studio was unveiled at Macromedia's UCON event in New York. The launch was backed by a host of names from the high-end offline 3D world, including Alias|wavefront, Discreet, Softimage and NewTek. Macromedia reiterated that the principal uses for the new technology would be games, entertainment, education and online shopping.

Users would view this content using the latest version of the Shockwave player, while designers would create it from scratch in Director 8.5, or import it from existing high-end 3D packages such as 3ds Max, Lightwave or Maya. The launch received widespread acclaim — not least because it truly looked like it would bring web 3D into the mainstream. At the time of the launch, more than 200 million web users had a copy of the Shockwave player installed on their system.

Designers quickly started to experiment with the new technology, and by May 2001, Macromedia was boasting about its use on high-profile sites such as CBS Sportsline, Fox Kids, Lego and National Geographic. In August, the company announced a deal to bundle Director 8.5 with 3ds Max, showing its ambition to woo traditional 3D modellers and animators onto the web. Meanwhile, in October, Macromedia responded to complaints about Director 8.5's shoddy documentation by releasing a series of video tutorials on its website. Then, in January 2002, it released a new version that included anti-aliasing support, which improved the visual quality of 3D objects and eliminated the unsightly jagged lines that are an unwanted feature of much 3D content. A native Mac OS X version of the Shockwave player was also released.

By the start of 2002, web designers were beginning to get to grips with Shockwave 3D, as you'll see from some of the case studies in this book. This has had a knock-on effect on users, with more than 300,000 people a day downloading the latest version of the Shockwave player. Since then, Macromedia has struck a deal with Intel to distribute the software with all the latter company's desktop motherboards.

ADOBE
Macromedia wasn't the only company working on a new web 3D technology at this time. In March 2001, Adobe unveiled Atmosphere, a new tool for creating 3D worlds for the web. The declamatory launch hype was reminiscent of VRML's heyday. 'Today, browsing a site means clicking on document links and doing simple searches', said Bruce Damer of the Digital Space Corporation, one of Adobe's supporters. 'In the near future, browsing a site will mean walking though 3-D room spaces, speaking with other visitors or site representatives, and seeing animated objects in real-time and in a more lifelike setting.'

Adobe released a public beta version of the Atmosphere authoring tool, enabling designers to get their hands on it for free and start experimenting. Within a month, more than 500,000 copies had been downloaded. At the same time, a beta version of the Atmosphere browser was made available for people to view the new content. Since then, Adobe has used the resulting feedback to fine-tune both applications, releasing a series of beta updates with new features and corrected bugs.

In contrast to Shockwave 3D, Atmosphere is being pitched specifically as a community-building tool. 'It's not game-focused, and it's not object-focused,' says Peder Engrob, who works at Adobe as a Web Evangelist. 'It's community-focused. We're focusing on how to build communities on the web

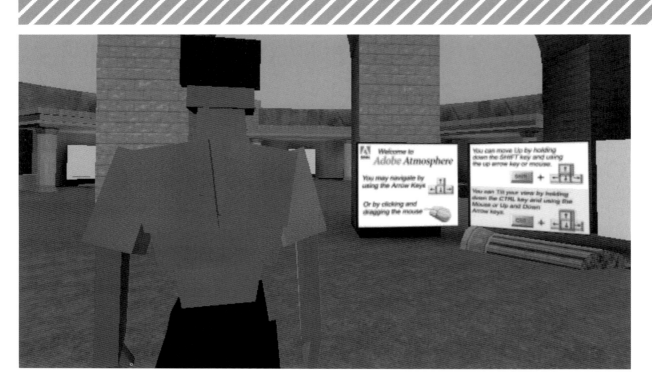

in 3D, with users creating their own personalized avatars. That's where we think the fun is.' Although this encompasses simple chatrooms, it also applies to the education market — Engrob cites virtual museums as an example, complete with sculptures and other 3D artworks. 'Users can walk around the museum, and look at these objects,' he says. 'But they can also discuss what they're seeing with other users who are doing the same.'

The Atmosphere Builder tool has been designed to be as accessible as possible to designers, most of whom will already be familiar with other Adobe products like Photoshop or Illustrator. It also uses JavaScript for its coding functions — a language that many web designers have been using for years. In theory, it's possible to have a workable 3D environment up and running within a day of downloading Atmosphere.

From a user's perspective, the Atmosphere browser is equally impressive. Its intelligent cacheing means that when you download a world, the first elements to appear are the basic 3D shapes that make it up. Once they've arrived, you can start to move around the environment as the textures, lighting, sounds and other elements download. If you're using a standard 56k modem, this is a boon — although downloading the 6Mb browser in the first place can be time-consuming.

Adobe's original plan was to release a commercial version of the Atmosphere Builder tool by Summer 2001. By the end of the year, it still hadn't appeared — at the time of writing this book, it is pencilled in for Summer 2002. Engrob explains the delay. 'We want to come out with Macintosh support and better hardware rendering support', he says. 'That's going to take time, though, because we want to do it right.' However, the delay has enabled more improvements to be made.

In December 2001, Adobe signed a deal with Havok to include its Hard Core Physics Engine with Atmosphere, introducing realistic real-world physics. In the same month, the firm announced the winners of its first Atmosphere contest, which was launched to spotlight the best of the first crop of worlds created using the tool.

By the time you read this, Atmosphere 1.0 should finally have been released. Designers have undoubtedly been impressed by it, but the big question is whether businesses will be too. Will clients who have been stung by web 3D's failures in the past be willing to pay designers to produce Atmosphere content? As you'd expect, Engrob is optimistic. 'Traditionally, it's been difficult for people to make revenue from 3D web projects', he concedes. 'But I think a lot of companies would like to have some kind of 3D profile on the web, so finally there's light at the end of the tunnel for products like Atmosphere. That's why Adobe's entering at this quite late stage. We couldn't have done this five years ago.'

VRML AND X3D
In a sense, Atmosphere is aiming at many of the same markets that VRML did back in 1996. It is tempting to assume that the latter technology died a death in the face of ignorance from internet users and businesses alike, but that's not entirely true. There is still an enthusiastic community of developers creating VRML worlds to be viewed in browsers such as Cortona or Blaxxun.

While many of the major VRML players abandoned the market years ago, some continued throughout the barren years. In March 2001, for example, Parallel Graphics created a site that allowed users to watch the final days of the Mir space station as it re-entered the Earth's atmosphere and broke up into debris. The firm used NASA data to plot the space station's position in real time, with visitors able to view it from various angles, as well as rotating and zooming in on the structure. According to Parallel Graphics, more than 40,000 people logged in to watch Mir's final hours.

VRML is alive and kicking then, but the Web3D Consortium which originally guided it has spent the last three years working on its next evolution: X3D. The process kicked off early in 1999, with executive director Deepak Kamlani explaining the aim of the new specification. '3D-based applications have been implemented in a number of different environments, particularly in the academic world and also in government', he said. 'It hasn't gone fully into the commercial market — and that's the attempt here: to make it more appealing for the commercial marketplace.'

X3D was finally unveiled in August 2001, and is essentially an updated version of VRML's last incarnation, albeit with a number of individual specs that support 3D applications on set-top boxes and mobile devices. The Consortium has been working closely with the MPEG-4 Group and the World Wide Web Consortium (W3C) to ensure that it gets industry backing, and in the latter case, to ensure that it integrates properly with XML. The new spec was launched with the support of key VRML companies such as Blaxxun, Parallel Graphics and OpenWorlds. The first new browsers started to appear

by the end of 2001, with backwards VRML compatibility an important element.

'Until there are exporters for things like 3ds Max and Lightwave, and browsers that are distributed widely, I'm not sure it'll reach any momentum', says Larry Rosenthal, who runs cube3.com. 'X3D is stuck in what killed VRML in 1997 — politics, people ego and no real cooperative marketing plans to make it a mass format targeted at creatives.'

LOOKING FORWARD
VRML and X3D continue to offer some intriguing possibilities, but it is the entry of Macromedia and Adobe into the market that makes me feel that web 3D is finally going to explode. There's a number of good development tools, and most internet users — in the developing world at least — are using 56k modems or even broadband connections. There is also a large base of talented designers from the worlds of web design and offline 3D modelling and animation.

All of this will be worthless if we can't find useful applications for web 3D. It's tempting to create 3D content simply for its own sake. What's more important, though, is that users want to use it, and where necessary, that businesses are prepared to pay for it. That's not to discourage experimentation — after all, it's the non-commercial projects that usually push the boundaries — but to ensure we don't make the same mistakes as we have in the past.

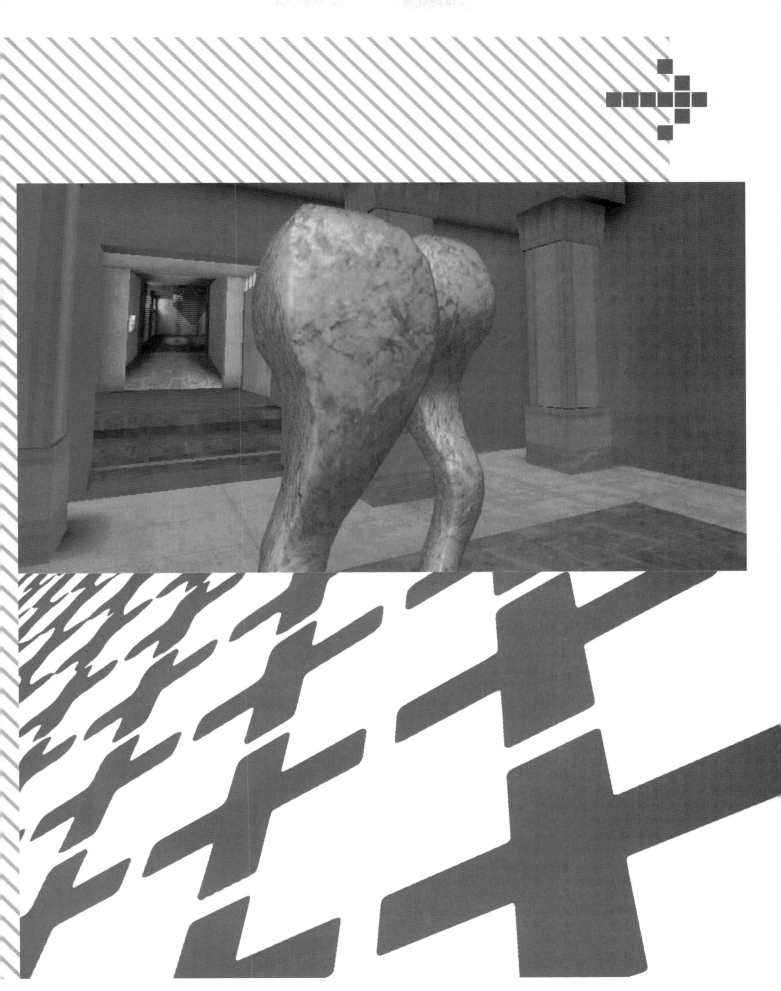

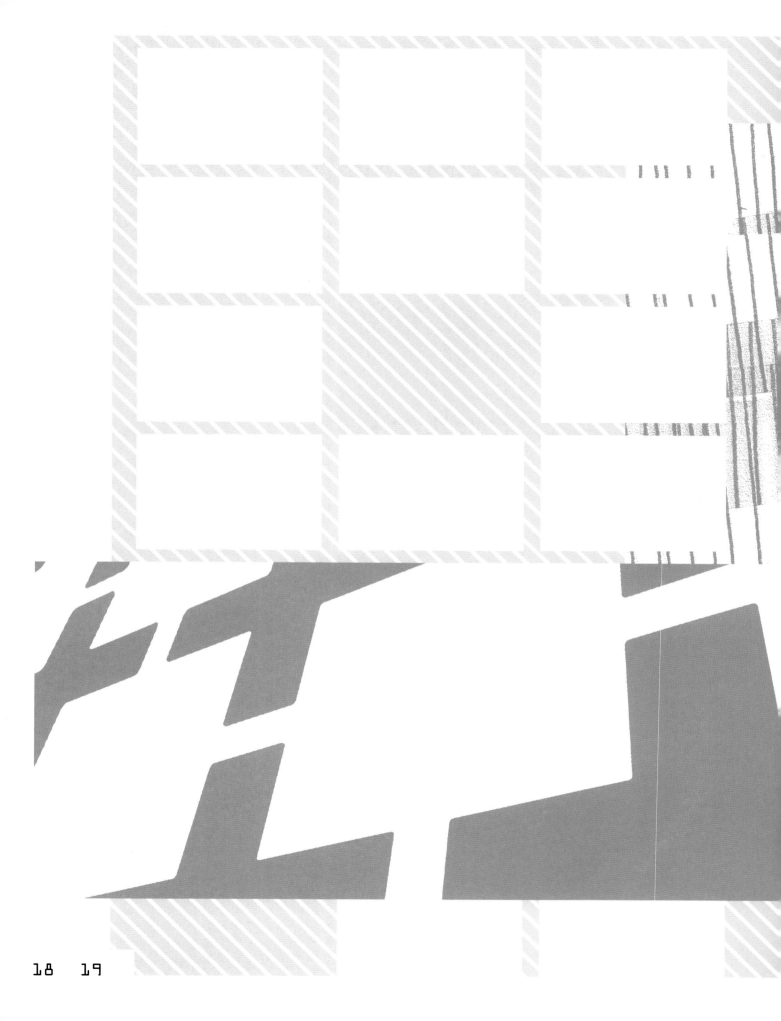

Whenever we use web 3D, it must be because it's better than the 2D alternatives. Would ecommerce sites really benefit from spinnable 3D products, or would a well-shot photograph suffice? Will people really want to wander round virtual houses when looking to buy property? Would kids really rather chat using a Quake-like first-person viewpoint rather than simple text? Sometimes the answer will be yes, sometimes it will be no. What's important is that designers are prepared to ask these questions.

The case studies in this book show how web 3D is already being used to great effect by designers around the world. Sometimes it's just one person working out of their home, or a small group of friends experimenting after hours. Meanwhile, companies like the Groove Alliance and WildTangent are developing new web 3D technologies, and then producing content that showcases them.

If you look at other 3D markets like games or CG movies, they are big-budget industries where large teams of designers work on multi-million dollar projects. By contrast, web 3D is in its infancy, yet that's what makes it such an exciting area. If you're a talented designer with some good ideas, the web is an increasingly attractive platform on which to distribute them. It may have under-achieved in the past, but in 2002, web 3D is finally ready to live up to its hype.

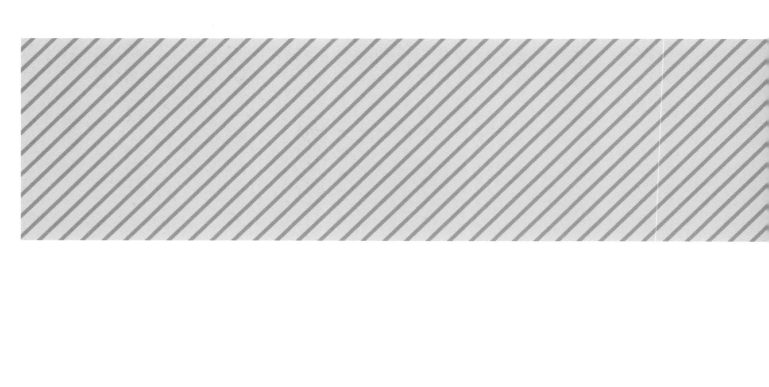

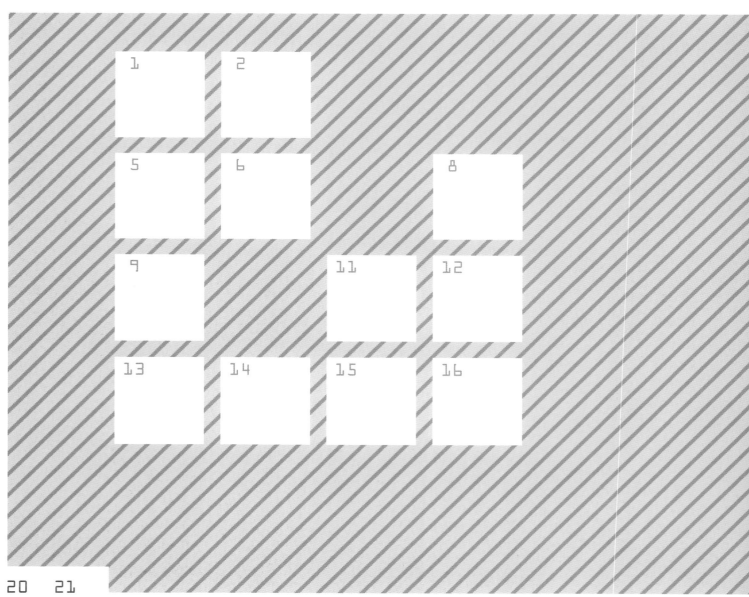

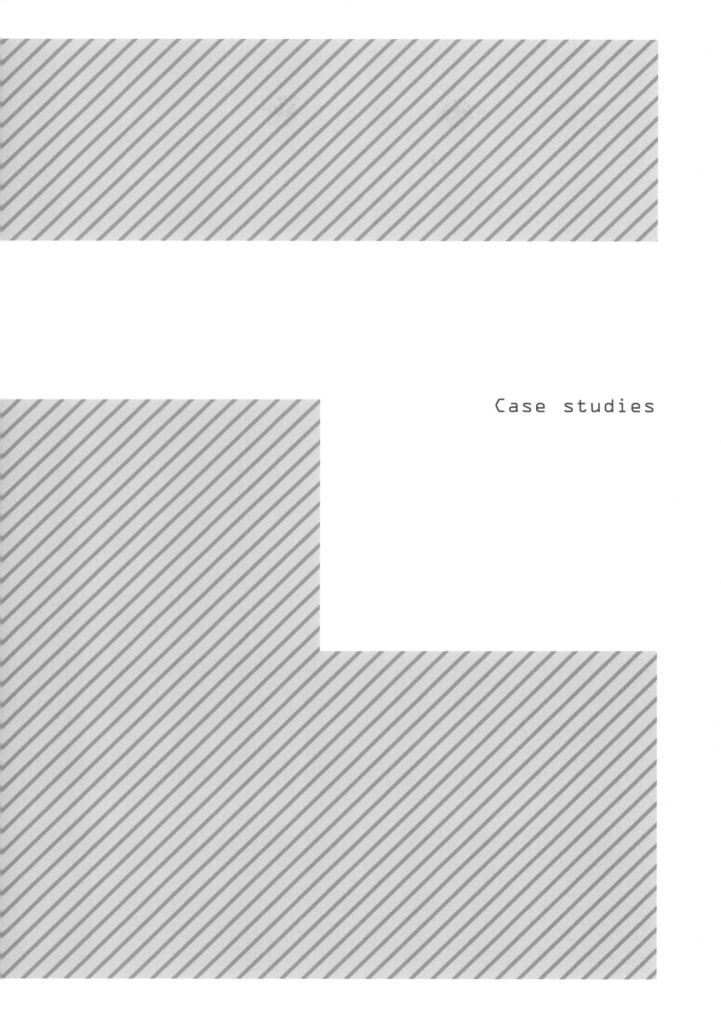

Case studies

HABBO HOTEL

www.habbohotel.com

Description: Chat environments
Agency: Sulake
Location: Finland
Launched: 1999–2000
Technology used: Shockwave, proprietary FUSE technology

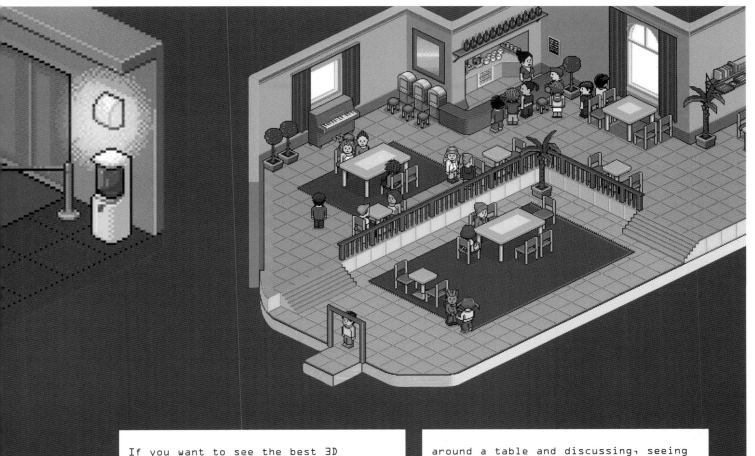

If you want to see the best 3D chatrooms currently on the web, you have to go to Finland. Well, not literally — you can simply log on. Back in August 1999, web designers Sampo Karjalainen and Aapo Kyrölä were asked to create a site for Mobiles, a Finnish rap band. Rather than create a standard music site, the pair decided to create a virtual retrogaming-style disco environment. 'We weren't really trying to build an online community in the first place', explains Sampo. 'The idea was just to make something interesting for the band. They finished quite soon, but the site started to live its own life. It worked so well, we wanted to continue working on the same kind of projects.'

Mobiles Disco quickly became a hangout for a generation of web designers, seduced by its distinctive visuals. It wasn't long before Sampo and Aapo, under their new agency name of Sulake, launched a next-generation version — Habbo Hotel — aimed at a more mainstream audience of web users. Both sites use the same 3D perspective, as Sampo explains. 'Spatiality is an important factor in Habbo and Mobiles Disco, it makes the place feel like a real social environment. Sitting

around a table and discussing, seeing other people in the room but not hearing them ... it's like a real-world cafe or bar. The visual influences for Mobiles Disco were Playmobil toys and old computer games like Head Over Heels. The stiffness of the Playmobil toys combined with the simple axonometric pixel graphics makes the style quite distinctive. If Mobiles Disco is reminiscent of Commodore 64 graphics, then Habbo Hotel is more like something on an Amiga 500. It's got the same foundation — hand-drawn pixel graphics and the perspective — but this time with more colours and some lighting effects.'

It's not just a visual thing though. Sulake built its own client-server system to use on Mobiles Disco, because at the time, the designers weren't impressed with Macromedia's own multi-user server. Sulake now has its own Java-based server, FUSE, which uses MySQL database. It enables the agency to run different rooms of Habbo Hotel on different servers, and add new hardware when needed. Sulake even provides an open-source version, FUSE Light, on its website for other designers to use.

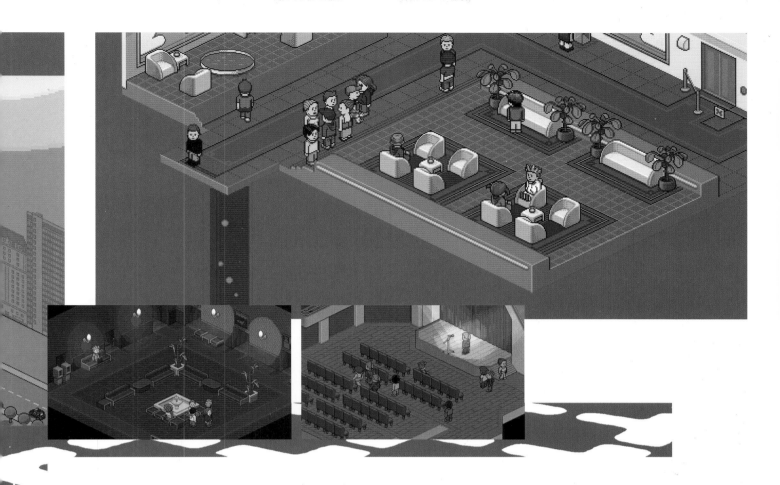

'The main issue is accessibility,'
says Sampo. 'It must be easy for the
user to get started. Once you learn
to use the interface and get some
friends, it makes sense to dig deeper
— get your own room, furnish it and
arrange different kinds of activities.
It's like climbing steps: you can't
ask the user to start a virtual life
on the front page. Most users just
want to check it out and have fun.'

The same goes for the technology,
which Sampo believes has to be as
seamless as possible. Currently, Habbo
Hotel uses Macromedia's Shockwave
plug-in, which, although highly
popular, isn't as widespread as Flash,
for example. 'Some people are still
not able to access it immediately,'
admits Sampo. 'But it's better than
proprietary client software, which
needs to be downloaded, installed and
maybe configured before you can enter
the environment.'

In the future, Sulake's intentions
are to work on projects where users
can have even more control over the
environment, building their own rooms

and authoring their own content.
Meanwhile, the agency is also working
on HUUHAA, its new client-server
technology for massive multi-player
online role-playing games, which will
use a similar 3D perspective. 'Instead
of a room-based approach, it supports
vast, continuous environments', he
says. 'We have the core of the game
engine up and running, and we're
planning to set up a pilot project
here in Finland.'

DARK CITY

www.hamonrye.com/atmosphere/

Description: Environment
Designer: George Lippert
Location: USA
Launched: 2001
Technology used: Adobe Atmosphere

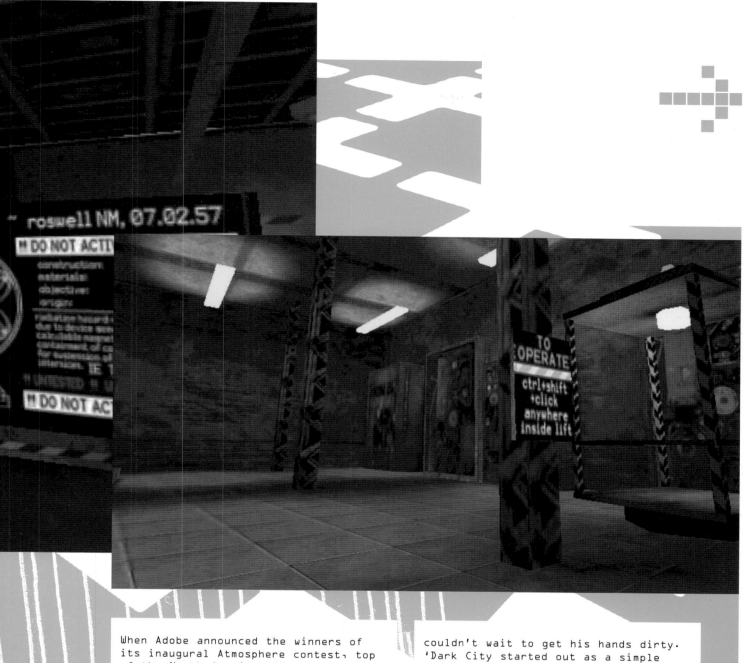

roswell NM, 07.02.57

When Adobe announced the winners of its inaugural Atmosphere contest, top of the North American list was Dark City. It is the work of George Lippert, a designer who works at a firm called Ham On Rye Technologies, building stereoscopic 3D animations for use in virtual reality goggles. In his spare time he created Dark City, truly a labour of love, from its authentically modelled US diner through to its creepy subway and eerie submarine.

Having dabbled with other web 3D technologies like Pulse 3D and Cult 3D in the past, George was intrigued when Atmosphere was first launched. He couldn't wait to get his hands dirty. 'Dark City started out as a simple excuse to experiment with the tool', he says. 'I started with the diner, and the exterior was intended to be merely a series of planar images outside the windows. As I continued to explore Atmosphere's possibilities, however, the exterior evolved.'

That's certainly true. George added more buildings, and created streets, signs and even taxicabs to fill out the city. Finally, he built the outer boardwalk, docks and lighthouse. By this time, his ambitions were beginning to outstrip even his own city limits. 'I began to have ideas

HAM ON RYE TECHNOLOGIES'

DARK CITY

AN Adobe ATMOSPHERE WORLD

[SHORTCUTS]

INSTRUCTIONS

WHERE TO GO IN DARK CITY

CONTACT US / REPORT A PROBLEM

- HAM ON RYE DINER
- DARK CITY
- UNDERGROUND
- SUBWAY
- HANGAR 13
- SPACE STATION NIMOY

for Atmosphere that would be completely incongruous to implement in Dark City', he says. 'I started to construct seven connected worlds, ranging from the submarine ride to the space station. The end result was a series of interconnected worlds on a scale far beyond the original intent.'

Having scooped the Adobe contest prize, George is now working on a series of other worlds — he is yet to decide how many, but it could be as many as ten. He'll be using a large amount of Javascripting to create more game-like environments, making users progress through each world to unlock the next one, just like levels in a console game. 'The basic theme is a haunted castle adventure', he says. Meanwhile, he's looking forward to the continued development of Atmosphere, although he'd like it to be more designer-friendly. 'For artist types like myself, programming is a bane', he winces.

He is also concerned about the inherent performance lag when your worlds are being accessed by other people, especially if they've gone overboard on creating their own 3D character. 'Even the best-optimized worlds can be reduced to unplayable drags by some joker user with a 3,000-poly avatar', he says. However, he admits that other users will often speak up in these situations, meaning that worlds effectively police themselves.

On the whole though, he is very impressed, and thinks the future is bright for Adobe's tool. 'Its potential has only just begun to be explored', he says. 'Web 3D is going to be a major element in the years to come, and Atmosphere is shaping up to be one of the standards of the industry. From product display to exciting chat environments, from the selling of homes via an exploratory online example to team gaming. The possibilities merely need to be tapped.'

INT3D

www.int3d.com

Description: Walkthrough technology
Firm: INT3D
Location: Italy
Launched: 2001
Technology used: Proprietary software

Web designers aren't all content to work with the technology created by firms like Macromedia and Adobe. Some are so keen to produce innovative web 3D content that they've coded their own tools. One such project is INT3D, which was unveiled at the end of 2001 by an Italian collective of designers, fired up by a passion for realtime 3D. It is a 3D editor that users can access online.

Targeted mainly at the interior design market, it allows users to create a room or house, place and move different kinds of furniture, vary the materials and colours, and then walk into the final 3D scene and interact with it. 'It's one of the more accessible 3D editors', says Gianni Dragone, one of the INT3D team. 'It works online, and to use it, all you have to do is install one of the advised VRML clients like Cortona, Cosmoplayer or Contact.' Although this makes it accessible to home users, it also has applications for commercial projects — for example, 3D walkthroughs for estate agents or building firms, putting it into the same category as

Parallel Graphics' Outline 3D technology. Alternatively, it could be used by manufacturers of furniture and domestic appliances. 'We can make interactive 3D models for these companies that are precise and accurate reproductions of their products, and insert them into our system', says Dragone.

One of the most important aspects of INT3D is the fast download of scenes created using it. 'It's no secret that the large size of 3D files has been one of the main problems for the application of 3D technology', says Dragone. 'Our project shows that it is possible to create excellent 3D scenes with the same file size as normal HTML pages with 2D graphics.' It's a real bonus for people using 56k modems — or lower — to access the web. By comparison, some of the more complicated Atmosphere worlds can take up to ten minutes to download through a slow connection.

Dragone thinks that web 3D has grown up fast in the last two years, thanks mainly to the increased computing

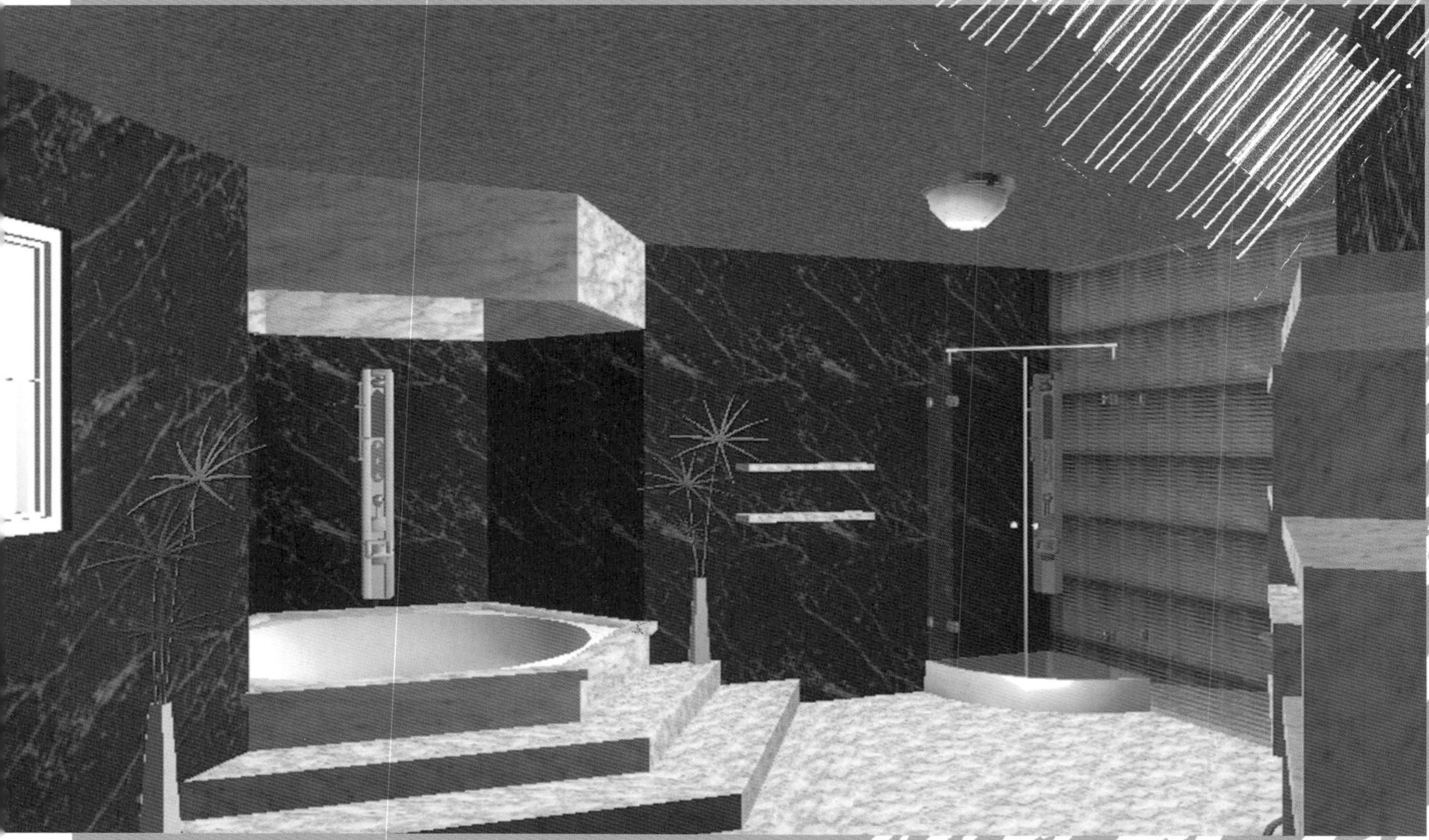

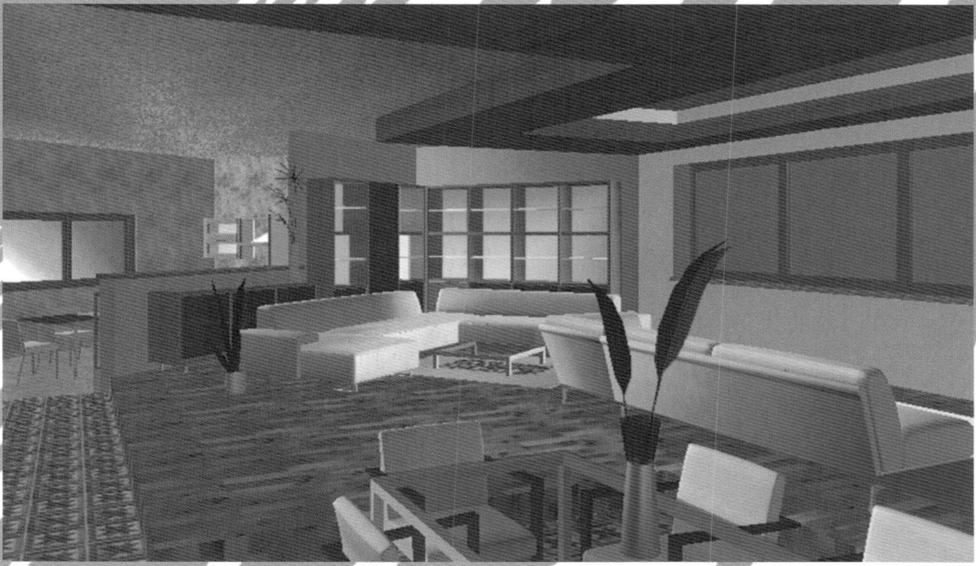

power of most home PCs. 'Processors
are more powerful, RAM is cheaper
and 3D accelerators are standard
components of most modern computers',
he says. 'All this enables people to
create complex and interesting VRML
projects. The most successful ones
currently are virtual manuals and
online teaching systems, but in
the future, we believe that VRML
technology will be applied with
success in many other fields.'

Recently, the INT3D team has been
optimizing its system, enlarging some
functions and simplifying others. It is
now ready to concentrate on promoting
the system and is considering its future
evolution. 'At the moment, INT3D is
mainly targeted at virtual buildings
and interiors', says Dragone. 'But on

the same basis, other similar tools
can be created in different fields. For
example, we are currently working on a
prototype of a 3D kitchen constructor,
through which users will be able to
create their own virtual kitchen.'

LEGO BRICK BUILDER

www.lego.com

Description: Various 3D content
Agency: Internal
Location: USA
Launched: 2001
Technology used: Flash

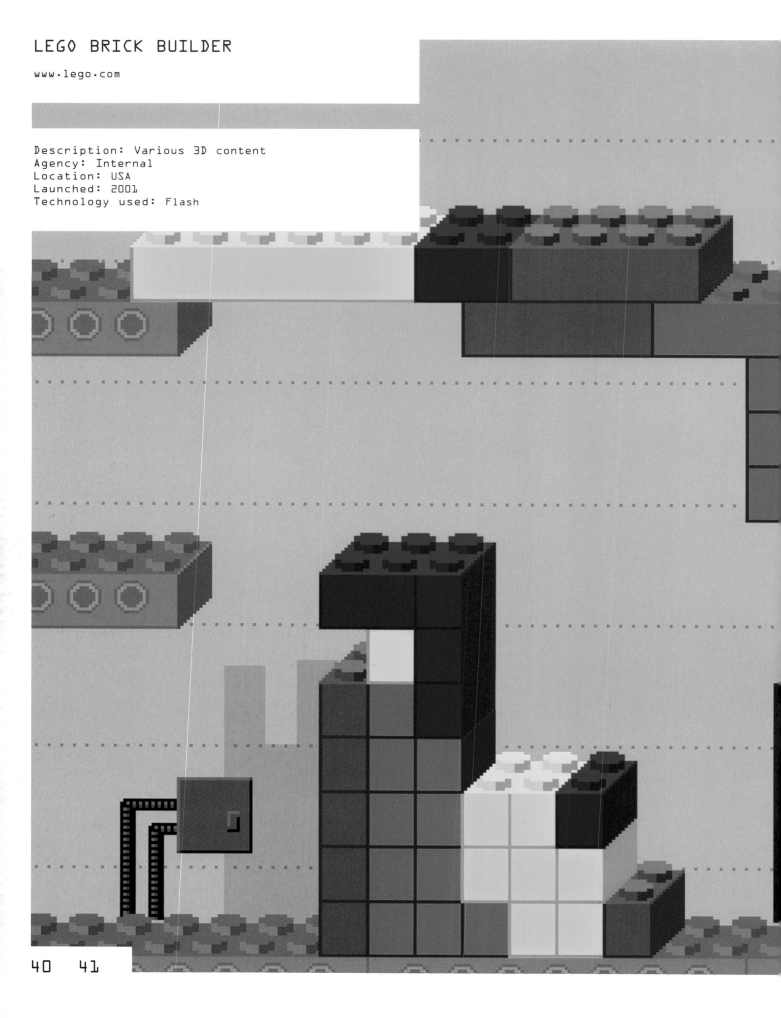

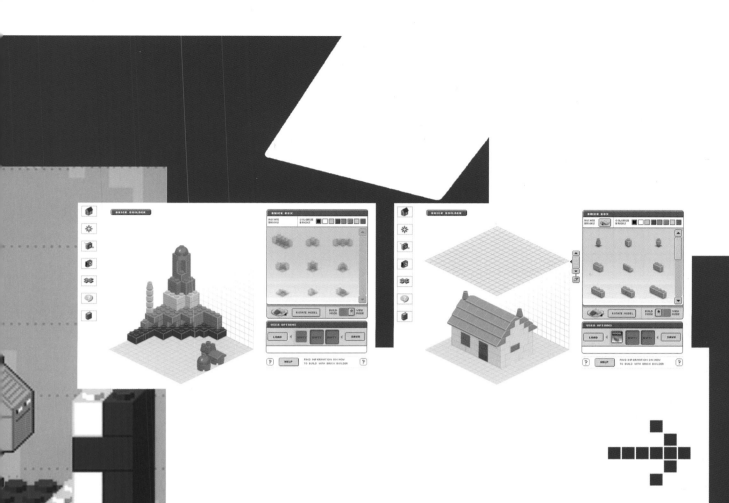

Like many children, when I was young, I had a big box of Lego. I used to spend hours building complex structures — and then much less time knocking them down again. But in time, I grew out of Lego, probably around the time I discovered computer games. The box of bricks was given away, to fulfil the same role in some other family. Yet here I am, twenty years later, constructing Lego buildings again. Except this time, the bricks are virtual, care of the Lego Brick Builder section of their official website.

The concept is simple — you log in, then use the simple drag'n'drop interface to build your own Lego creation. The Lego Brick Builder is a thing of beauty, with a simple Flash interface that belies the complex options available once you get stuck in. Naturally, it's probably the site's core audience of children who are making the most of it, but I'm fairly sure that it attracts a healthy number of adults like me, too, lured by nostalgic memories of our former Lego skills.

The Lego Brick Builder is a good example of cutting-edge Flash 3D development, as creatives push Macromedia's tool to the limit, rather than use the weightier Shockwave technology. You're not left waiting for the Builder application to download, while changes such as rotating your creation happen immediately. You don't need complex instructions to work out how to use it, as the interface is accessible and intuitive. And with a few simple touches — you can save your creations when you've finished them, for example — the designers have ensured that users will come back again and again to the site.

Overall, Lego.com has been one of the most high-profile websites to try new kinds of 3D content. Besides the Brick Builder, there's a host of other Lego-related 3D games for visitors to play.

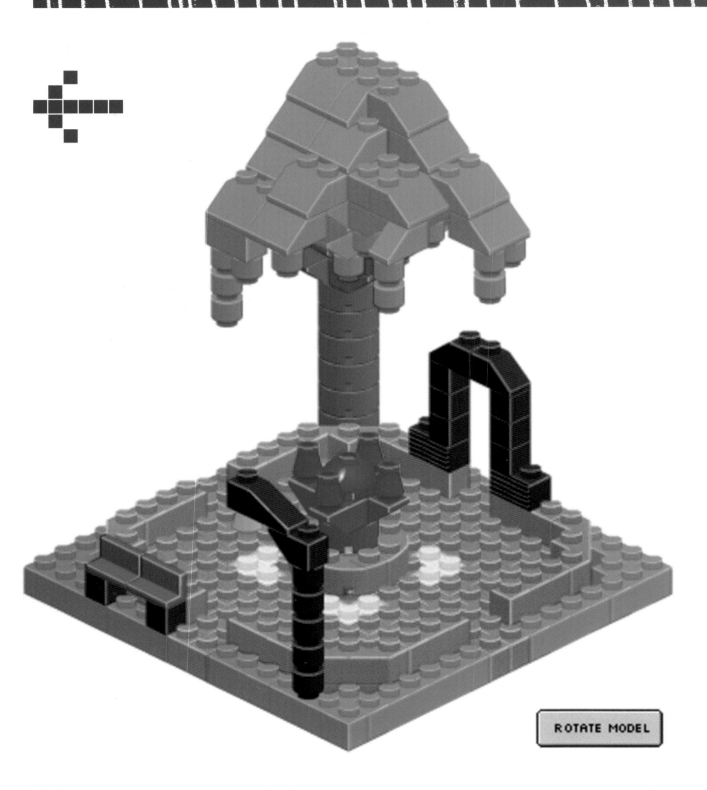

ROTATE MODEL

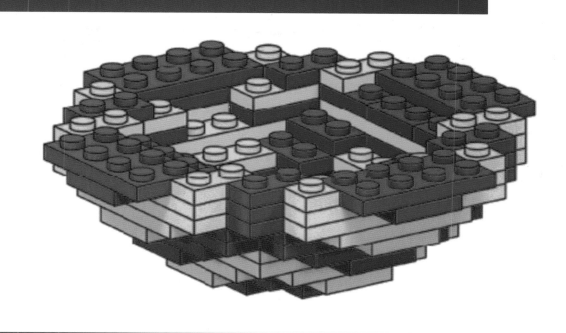

In 2001, Lego.com was one of the first sites to commit to Macromedia's new Shockwave 3D technology, with the launch of a game called Robohunter 2: Spy City, which saw players exploring a shadowy 3D city to find a spy. Since then, it has been followed by a series of other Shockwave 3D games. 'We're always looking for better ways to bring the sheer fun of playing with Lego products into the online space', said Russell Stoll, the creative director at Lego's online division. 'Shockwave opens up amazing new possibilities in that area.'

Lego is a company that has built its offline reputation around a product that's inherently 3D — coloured bricks. So it's no surprise to find the firm making the most of web 3D technologies to knit together its online community of users. Besides developing the Builder and commissioning more games, it's clear that there is a lot of potential for further 3D applications. For example, instructions for building complex Lego models, complete with 3D animations to guide you every step of the way. One thing's for sure: it is sites like this that will pave the way for others to follow in their 3D footsteps.

3D GROOVE

www.3dgroove.com

Description: 3D gaming technology
Agency: The Groove Alliance
Location: USA
Launched: 1999
Technology used: Proprietary engine

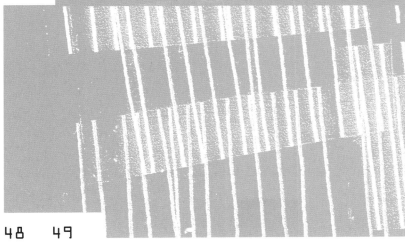

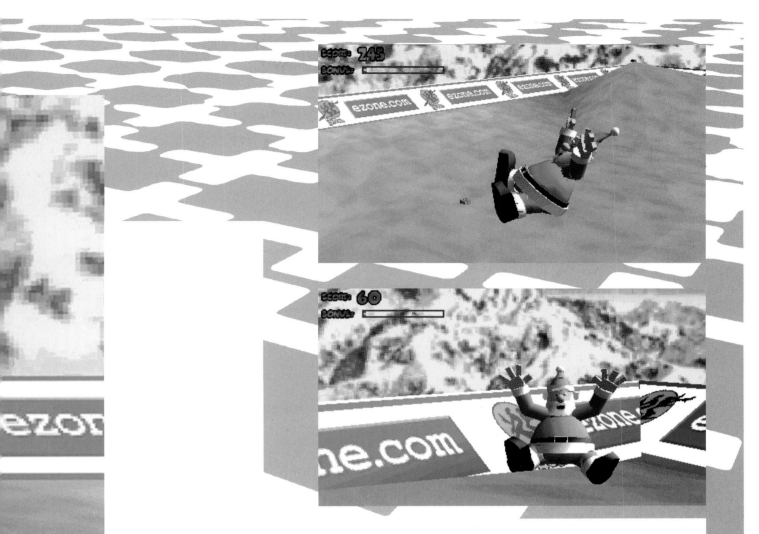

3D Groove isn't a website; it's a 3D games engine created by an American company called the Groove Alliance. It was founded by Jules Urbach, a games developer who famously dropped out of Harvard two weeks into his course to pursue a full-time career in the games industry. Among his hits was Hellcab, one of the first ever CD-ROM games. Now, the technology created by his company is driving the current generation of web 3D games.

'The key to our technology is that the development tools enable really easy and rapid development of games that are high-quality and fun to play', says Joseph Varet, Groove Alliance VP of business development. 'You wouldn't want to create Gran Turismo 3 with them, but if you've got $50—100k to produce a web game in one to three months, it's perfect.'

The company started off by developing its own games. Its first title, Real Pool, was launched on Shockwave.com

in 1999, and within a year was being played more than a million times a month by gamers around the world. However, the company's business model has since evolved, to the point where it creates technology, rather than games per se. It now maintains a network of developers to whom it supplies the 3D Groove toolset for free.

Clients commission games from the Groove Alliance, which then hires one of its partner developers to do the job, and takes a cut of the fee. There are currently Groove-powered games on a range of major websites, including Warner Brothers, Nickelodeon and Cartoon Network. 'One thing we like about the medium is that we can create games that wouldn't be viable on a console platform', says Varet. 'We can take more risks, and really explore the boundaries of what can be done in 3D gaming.'

3D Groove's main appeal is that it enables great-looking games to be

created that download quickly, even over a 56k modem. The company even employs two dedicated engineers to focus on compression, allowing games to be squeezed down to the smallest possible file size. In the future, broadband will increase the possibilities. 'Dial-up will continue to be important for the forseeable future,' says Varet. 'So developers will have to be creative and resourceful. But broadband will be an opportunity to add more and more richness. We're incorporating scaling architecture into Groove 2 so we can dynamically call broadband or non-broadband assets depending on what connection a user is on.'

Varet explains that the key philosophy behind the Groove Alliance is to create a 'broadcasting' technology for video games, providing an alternative means of distribution to boxed software in shops — in much the same way that radio and television works for the music and video industries. 'Look at how the broadcasting business is bigger than the film business', he points out. 'Could that happen here? Maybe.'

The Groove Alliance has recently been preparing its second-generation software, Groove 2.0, as well as setting its sights on non-PC areas such as PDAs and set-top boxes. However, Varet is clear about the most important factor in the company's continued success — developer realization of the differences between web games and the console market. 'PS2 owners want games that take twenty hours to complete', he says. 'Our users are looking for something they can pick up quickly and be engaged by straight away. It's a five to fifteen-minute experience, but again and again. Our games are to traditional console games what a sitcom is to a feature film.'

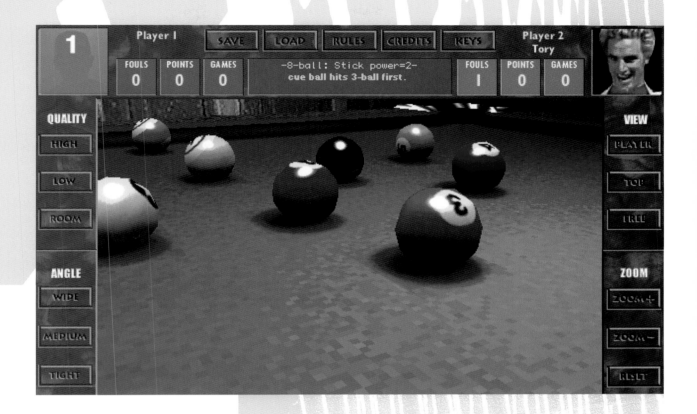

1	Player 1	SAVE	LOAD	RULES	CREDITS	KEYS	Player 2 Tory	

FOULS	POINTS	GAMES	-8-ball: Stick power=2-	FOULS	POINTS	GAMES
0	0	0	cue ball hits 3-ball first.	1	0	0

QUALITY

HIGH

LOW

ROOM

ANGLE

WIDE

MEDIUM

TIGHT

VIEW

PLAYER

TOP

FREE

ZOOM

ZOOM+

ZOOM−

RESET

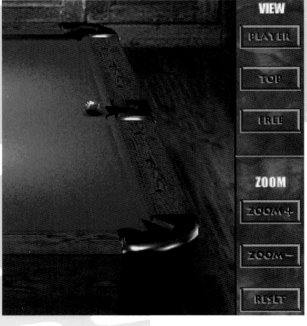

VIEW

PLAYER

TOP

FREE

ZOOM

ZOOM+

ZOOM−

RESET

HORSES FOR COURSES

www.thequality.com/horsesforcourses/en/index.html

Description: 3D interactive movie
Agency: thequality.com
Location: UK
Launched: 2000
Technology used: 3ds Max, Photoshop, b3d Studio

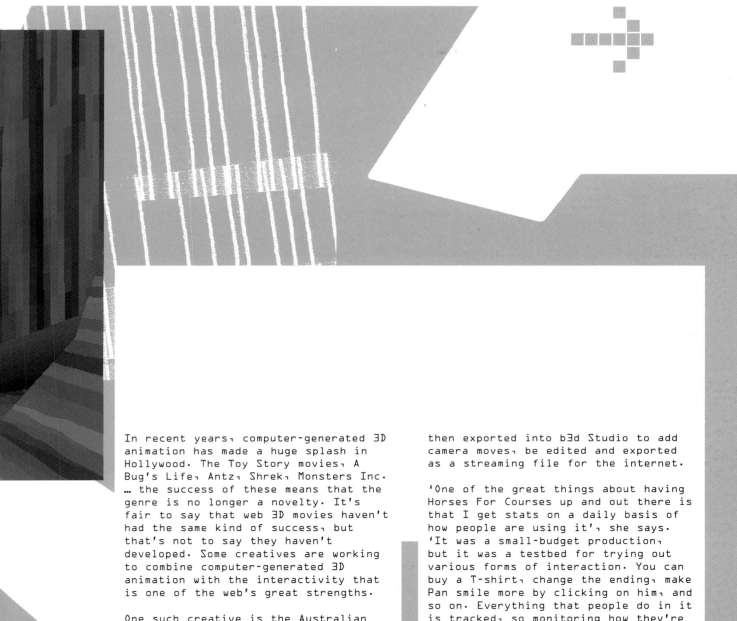

In recent years, computer-generated 3D animation has made a huge splash in Hollywood. The Toy Story movies, A Bug's Life, Antz, Shrek, Monsters Inc. … the success of these means that the genre is no longer a novelty. It's fair to say that web 3D movies haven't had the same kind of success, but that's not to say they haven't developed. Some creatives are working to combine computer-generated 3D animation with the interactivity that is one of the web's great strengths.

One such creative is the Australian designer, Michela Ledwidge, and her agency thequality.com. Having been involved in online production since the earliest days of the web — in 1993 she set up the first web server in Sydney, Australia — in 2001 her short film Horses For Courses won the Web3D Best Animation prize at the SIGGRAPH trade show. It's a dreamlike fairy tale in which Pan, the god of nature, comes face-to-face with the modern world. The movie's 3D elements were created using 3ds Max, while the 2D elements and textures were handled in Photoshop. The finished 3D scenes were then exported into b3d Studio to add camera moves, be edited and exported as a streaming file for the internet.

'One of the great things about having Horses For Courses up and out there is that I get stats on a daily basis of how people are using it', she says. 'It was a small-budget production, but it was a testbed for trying out various forms of interaction. You can buy a T-shirt, change the ending, make Pan smile more by clicking on him, and so on. Everything that people do in it is tracked, so monitoring how they're interacting gives me an inkling as to what my next project will be.'

There's one criticism that Michela levels at her own film — it's not truly cross-platform. Using the b3d technology means that Mac users can only view a video version, rather than the truly interactive version. This wasn't a deliberate decision — at the time Horses For Courses was made, b3d was intending to roll out a Mac version of its technology. But it gave Michela a lesson to take forward. 'I'm very interested in exploring web 3D's

potential for real communication on a wide scale', she says. 'Not being restricted to one platform or browser is really important. I'm doing quite a lot of stuff now with Shockwave 3D, because it's cross-platform.'

Recently, Michela has been presenting Horses For Courses at various conferences, as well as plotting her next project. She's also working on an ambitious idea for a club event involving multiple screens, SMS texting and a 3D virtual compere. She remains optimistic about the future for web 3D. 'My interest in it isn't just because it's colourful and game-like, but because when you're talking about building stuff on the fly in response to user interaction, it's the ultimate dynamic medium.'

More than that, though, she thinks Horses For Courses represents a new approach to film-making that could one day shake up Hollywood's way of doing things. 'The open-source approach to film-making is going to grow from the web. In the film industry, everything is behind locked doors and jealously

guarded. But if you look at something like Flash on the web, some of the most famous designers came to prominence because they did cool stuff, and then put the source files up on the web so other people could learn from them. We'll be doing the same.'

TOPLAY SOCCER

www.plus.es/futbol3D/default.asp

Description: 3D football highlights
Agency: Orad and Intel Architecture Lab
Location: Spain
Launched: 2000
Technology used: OradNet TOPlay, Shockwave 3D

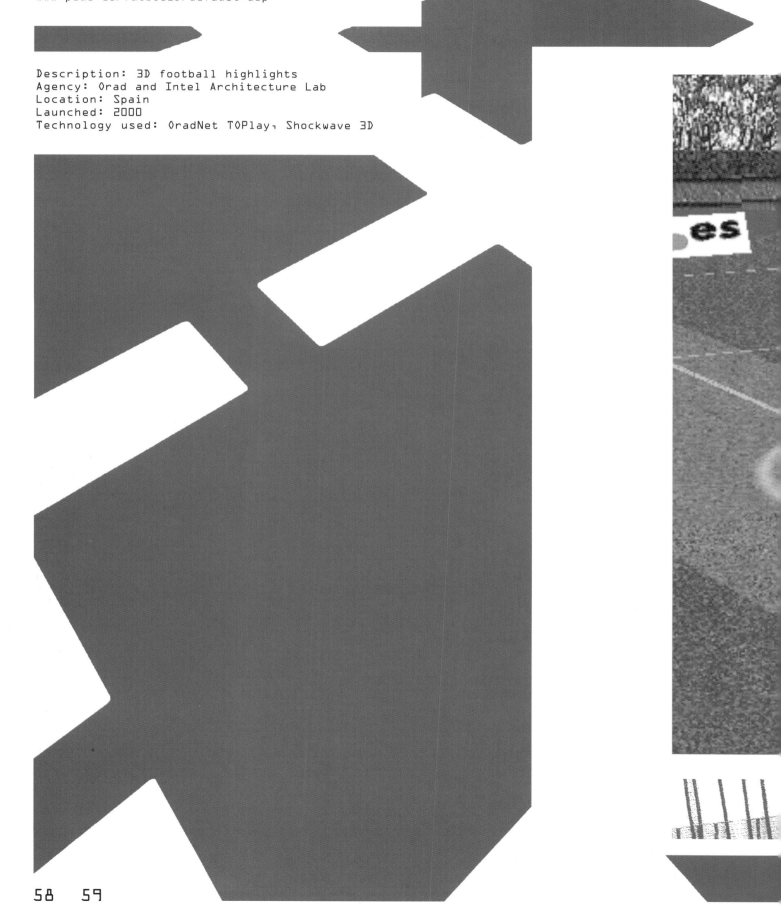

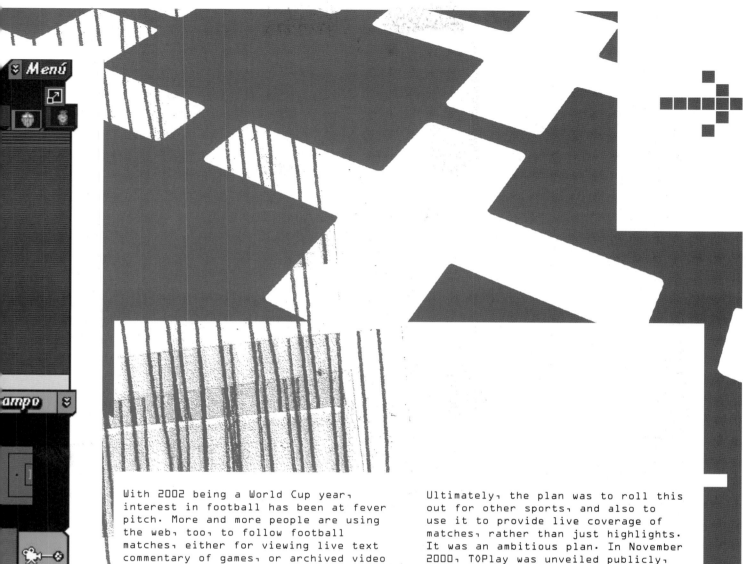

With 2002 being a World Cup year, interest in football has been at fever pitch. More and more people are using the web, too, to follow football matches, either for viewing live text commentary of games, or archived video highlights. You might think this is an area where web 3D has little place, but one project that was launched in 2000 seemed to prove otherwise.

The technology was called TOPlay, and was developed jointly by Israeli technology firm Orad and Intel's Architecture Lab (IAL). In August 2000 Orad created a dedicated spin-off subsidiary, OradNet (www.oradnet.com), to develop web 3D technologies. The aim was to create a tool that could generate 3D graphical simulations of soccer highlights. 'For instance, soccer fans seeking a more personal view of a match would now be able to enjoy a graphical visualization of a match by choosing their viewpoint', said OradNet CEO Zack Keinan at the time. 'They could choose to watch the match through the eyes of their favourite player, for example.'

Ultimately, the plan was to roll this out for other sports, and also to use it to provide live coverage of matches, rather than just highlights. It was an ambitious plan. In November 2000, TOPlay was unveiled publicly, using Macromedia's Shockwave technology to display the highlights. It received widespread publicity, and by April 2001, OradNet was reportedly negotiating with clubs such as Manchester United and Liverpool to make the system available on their official websites.

OradNet even produced a demo of Diego Maradona's infamous handball 'goal' against England in the 1986 World Cup, to prove that TOPlay could be used to replay controversial incidents from a variety of angles. 'A system like ours could put an end to disputes between fans over key moments in a game', said Aya Evan, OradNet's marketing director. 'It can give the fans an insight into the game that they don't currently have. They can see the game through the eyes of a player, or the referee, for example.'

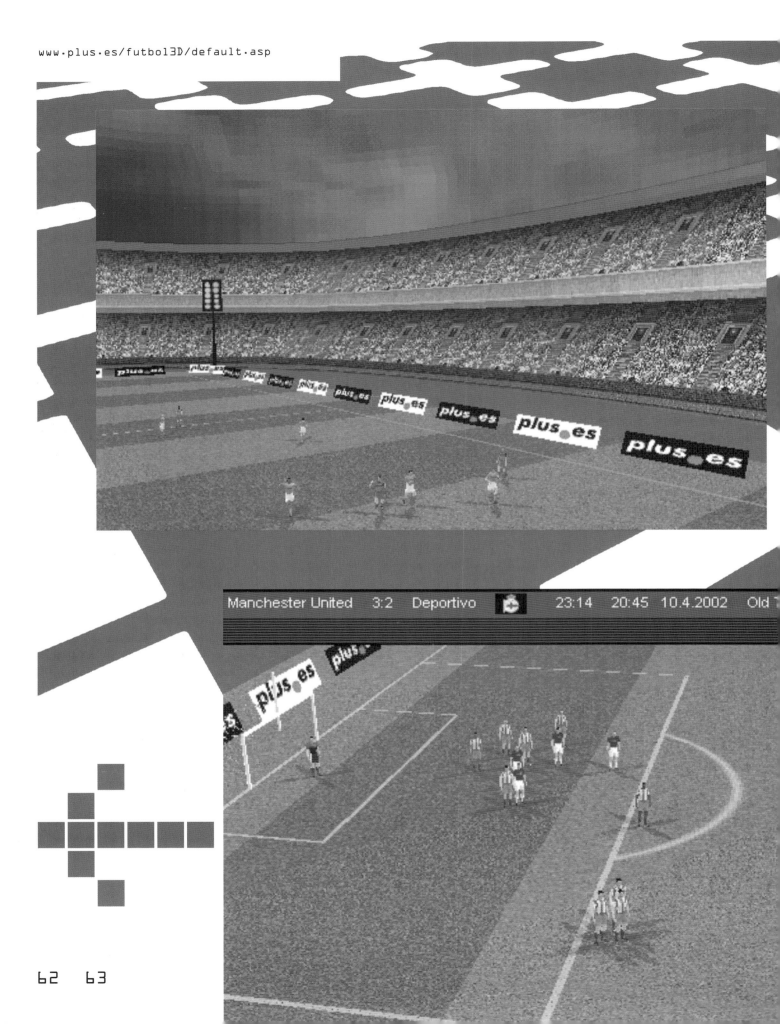

Manchester United   3:2   Deportivo   23:14   20:45   10.4.2002   Old T

One of the first sites to actually try out TOPlay was Spanish portal Plus.es, which provided its users with TOPlay highlights of games in the Spanish league and European Champions League. Using it, you can see just how much potential there is for this immersive sports technology. The self-contained TOPlay player is fairly easy to use, making it simple to switch perspectives on the action, as well as rewinding it to specific points.

At the time of writing, OradNet seems to have gone quiet, but I hope we have not heard the last from this technology. A possible application is on mobile phones, when the third-generation network (3G) arrives. 3G mobile operators have been promising video sports highlights as one of the services they'll be able to provide, but it's thought that this may not be possible for a few years yet. In the meantime, perhaps 3D Shockwave highlights — which require less bandwidth — could be an option. Its success depends, however, on the complex area of rights — who owns the online rights to sports footage and

whether they apply to 3D animations produced using them. Nevertheless, TOPlay is an ambitious 3D technology that deserves to play some role in the web of the next few years.

Description: 3D animated comic strips
Firm: Cool Beans Productions
Location: UK
Launched: 2001
Technology used: Maya, Renderman

"ONE DAY THE WORLD WILL KNOW MY NAME."

DR. KRIEGER

www.COOLBEANSWORLD.com

A demon with a terrible and secret past has had his soulless eyes fixed on the small town of Saintly for generations.

Hiding in the shadows and places not meant for humans, Jediah is quietly building an army of...things.

When people start to mysteriously disappear from the town, his dark agenda begins.

He knows their secrets,
their desires,
their fears.

Soon it will be time...

"Satan with a Southern drawl?"

JEDIAH T KANE

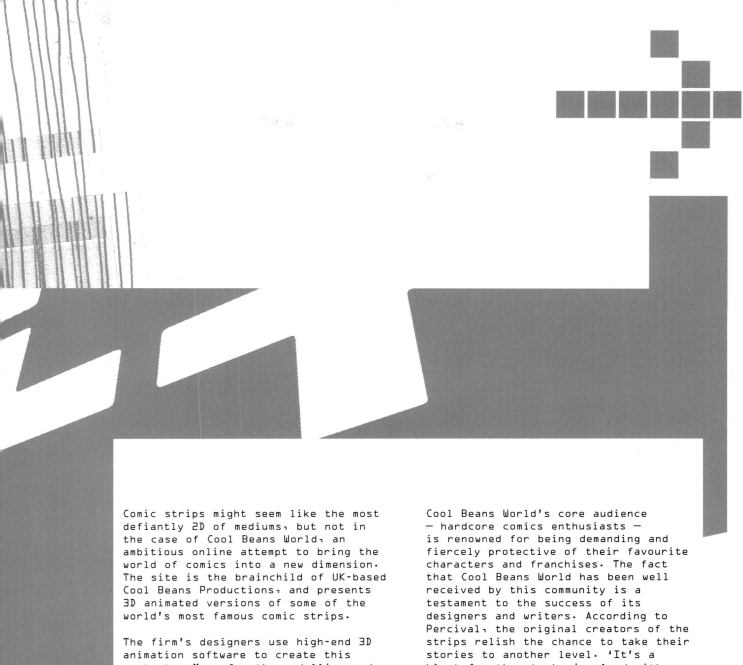

Comic strips might seem like the most defiantly 2D of mediums, but not in the case of Cool Beans World, an ambitious online attempt to bring the world of comics into a new dimension. The site is the brainchild of UK-based Cool Beans Productions, and presents 3D animated versions of some of the world's most famous comic strips.

The firm's designers use high-end 3D animation software to create this content — Maya for the modelling and Renderman for the rendering. They are the same tools used to create cutting-edge CG movies like Monsters Inc. and Shrek. 'We've been beta testing these for a number of years, so we have a good understanding of the software', says creative director Nick Percival. 'We combine these with a number of our own proprietary animation and texturing techniques. It's very powerful software, and with our 3D modellers and animators involved, it allows us to create the high-detail computer-animated comic book style that we're after.'

Cool Beans World's core audience — hardcore comics enthusiasts — is renowned for being demanding and fiercely protective of their favourite characters and franchises. The fact that Cool Beans World has been well received by this community is a testament to the success of its designers and writers. According to Percival, the original creators of the strips relish the chance to take their stories to another level. 'It's a blast for them to be involved with this format. It gives them a chance to direct their own mini-movies. The writer can now script in things like effects and camera movements to strengthen the narrative, while the artists are producing the storyboards and character designs. They're ecstatic to see their creations brought to life in 3D.'

This process brings challenges, though, not least of which is ensuring the spirit of the original comic strips is maintained online. 'A lot of these characters have only been designed with the 2D comics medium in mind', says Percival, citing Marshal Law as

Smart and opinionated with a keen baseball pitching hand, Mary Lou hangs out with Pug, Porky and Mr.Buggs, her toy bunny.

Her family have lived in Saintly for generations, but why do her parents go quiet when she mentions the gravedigger on Stalk Hill?

And did Mr.Buggs just wink at her a moment ago?

"It's a girl thing, doofus!"

MARY LOU BAXTER

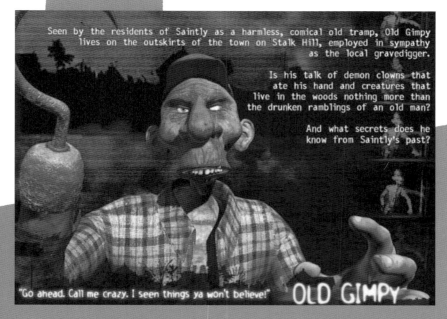

Seen by the residents of Saintly as a harmless, comical old tramp, Old Gimpy lives on the outskirts of the town on Stalk Hill, employed in sympathy as the local gravedigger.

Is his talk of demon clowns that ate his hand and creatures that live in the woods nothing more than the drunken ramblings of an old man?

And what secrets does he know from Saintly's past?

"Go ahead. Call me crazy. I seen things ya won't believe!"

OLD GIMPY

a prime example. 'We have to take
in all the quirks and style of the
original artists, and create convincing,
recognizable versions of their
characters as moving 3D images. It
takes a lot of work, but the results
are worth it. It gives the characters
a distinctive unique look.'

Cool Beans has ambitious plans for the
future, including an expansion into
mediums other than the web. Percival
thinks mobile devices will be another
delivery mechanism for all sorts of
electronic entertainment. 'There's
great potential for new forms of
episodic storytelling on these
devices', he says. 'We're currently
developing a series with this format
in mind.'

On the web front, he's also keen to
bring more interactivity into the Cool
Beans offering. The firm has already
done some test work on an animated
interactive comic strip, which
Percival thinks has great potential.
'It's a lot of work for the writer.
The storyline can take many different
twists and turns, but you still have

to keep a consistent narrative.
However, this would be a truly unique
form of storytelling that is still
backed up by all the things that
make good comics so cool — strong
plotlines, compelling characters and
great visuals.'

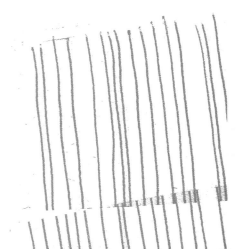

TEMPLE OF HEAVEN

www.wlv.ac.uk/~in6716/temple/TempleofHeaven.htm

Description: Environment
Designer: Li Jin
Location: UK
Launched: 2001
Technology used: Adobe Atmosphere

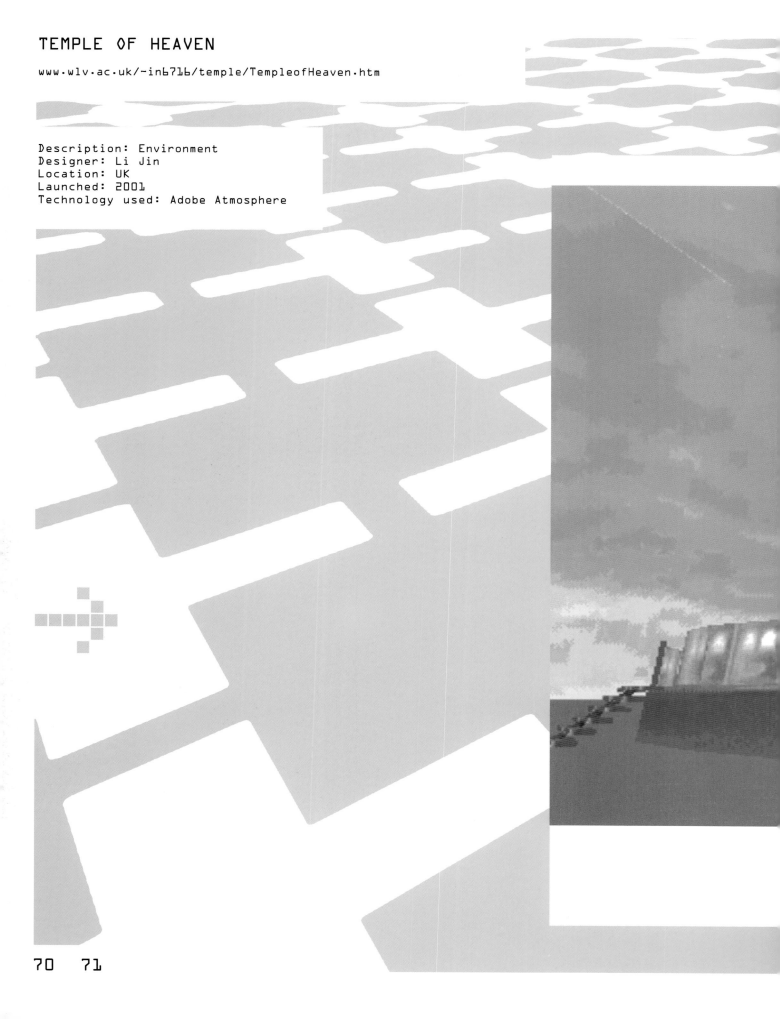

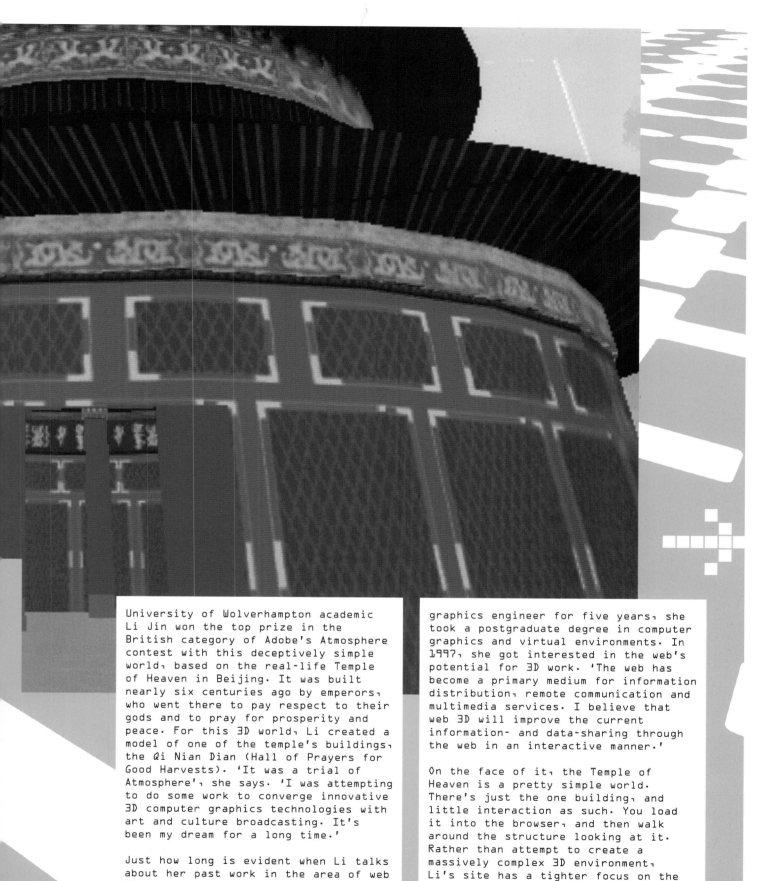

University of Wolverhampton academic Li Jin won the top prize in the British category of Adobe's Atmosphere contest with this deceptively simple world, based on the real-life Temple of Heaven in Beijing. It was built nearly six centuries ago by emperors, who went there to pay respect to their gods and to pray for prosperity and peace. For this 3D world, Li created a model of one of the temple's buildings, the Qi Nian Dian (Hall of Prayers for Good Harvests). 'It was a trial of Atmosphere', she says. 'I was attempting to do some work to converge innovative 3D computer graphics technologies with art and culture broadcasting. It's been my dream for a long time.'

Just how long is evident when Li talks about her past work in the area of web 3D. Having worked as a 3D computer graphics engineer for five years, she took a postgraduate degree in computer graphics and virtual environments. In 1997, she got interested in the web's potential for 3D work. 'The web has become a primary medium for information distribution, remote communication and multimedia services. I believe that web 3D will improve the current information- and data-sharing through the web in an interactive manner.'

On the face of it, the Temple of Heaven is a pretty simple world. There's just the one building, and little interaction as such. You load it into the browser, and then walk around the structure looking at it. Rather than attempt to create a massively complex 3D environment, Li's site has a tighter focus on the intricacies of this holy temple. It

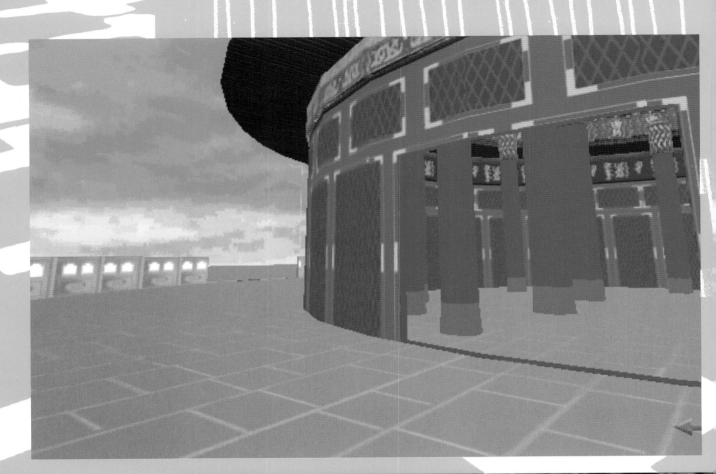

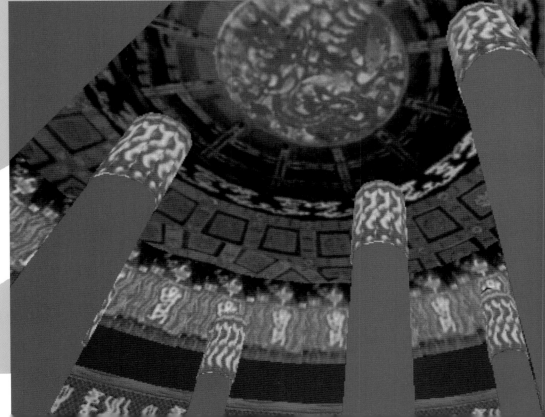

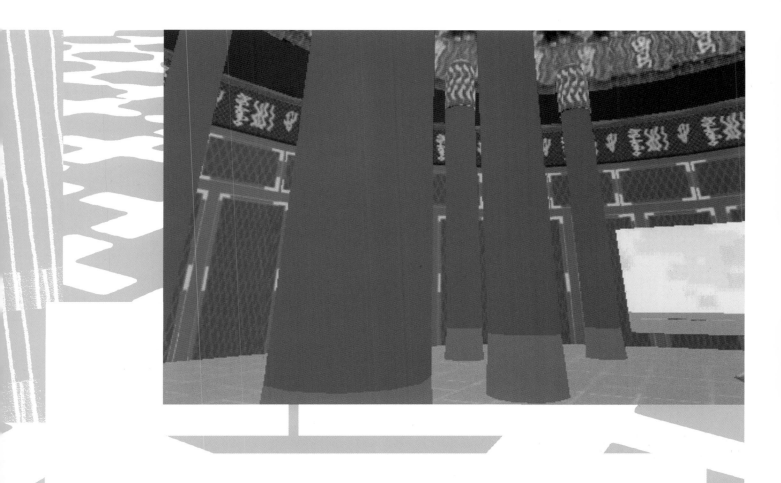

looks plain from afar, but get closer and look at the ceiling, and you can see the effort that's gone into it.

Li is impressed with Atmosphere's qualities as an environment-building tool. 'Its advantage is that it provides a high-level interface-friendly tool for artists to build and explore 3D content on the web, with no need for computer programming', she says. However, she also recognizes its flaws. 'The current beta version is still too weak to build complex 3D scenes. For example, it can't support various 3D file formats' conversion and arbitrary behaviours. Also, the interactive capability between users and 3D scenes is still very weak. It will take time to evolve.'

Li's future ambitions lie in the education sector. 'The rapid development of the web has already begun to foster collaborative information discovery and visual exploration', she says. 'Using standard web browsers as execution engines for web-based virtual reality will help the web to increasingly become the most common location for

VR applications. My personal ambitions are to apply web 3D to interdisciplinary research and applications such as online classical and ancient heritage, as well as 3D civilization reconstruction. Also, architecture design and viewing, scientific visualization and even ecommerce.'

She is also convinced that Atmosphere will continue to be important, and believes it will become more powerful and yet also easier for designers to use. 'I have every confidence it will be a success. I think it will be a big market, since nobody can refuse the charm of 3D, and the convenience of information-sharing through the web.'

MINI USA

www.miniusa.com

Description: 3D visualization
Agency: Euro RSCG Circle
Location: USA
Launched: 2001
Technology used: Flash, Quicktime

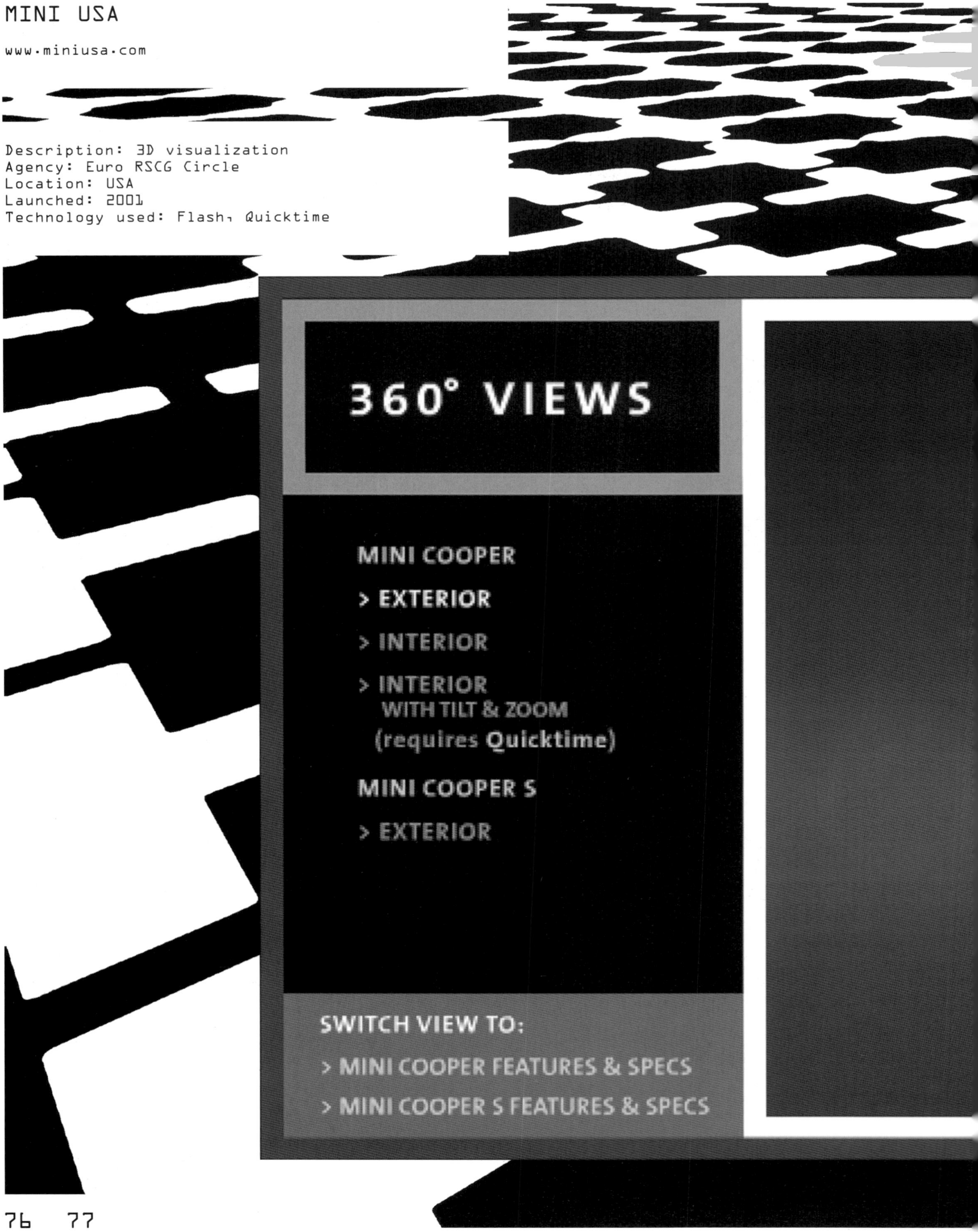

360° VIEWS

MINI COOPER

> **EXTERIOR**

> INTERIOR

> INTERIOR
WITH TILT & ZOOM
(requires **Quicktime**)

MINI COOPER S

> EXTERIOR

SWITCH VIEW TO:

> MINI COOPER FEATURES & SPECS

> MINI COOPER S FEATURES & SPECS

360° VIEWS

MINI COOPER
> **EXTERIOR**
> INTERIOR
> INTERIOR
  WITH TILT & ZOOM
  (requires **Quicktime**)
MINI COOPER S
> EXTERIOR

SWITCH VIEW TO:
> MINI COOPER FEATURES & SPECS
> MINI COOPER S FEATURES & SPECS

360° VIEWS

MINI COOPER
> EXTERIOR
> **INTERIOR**
> INTERIOR
  WITH TILT & ZOOM
  (requires **Quicktime**)
MINI COOPER S
> EXTERIOR

SWITCH VIEW TO:
> MINI COOPER FEATURES & SPECS
> MINI COOPER S FEATURES & SPECS

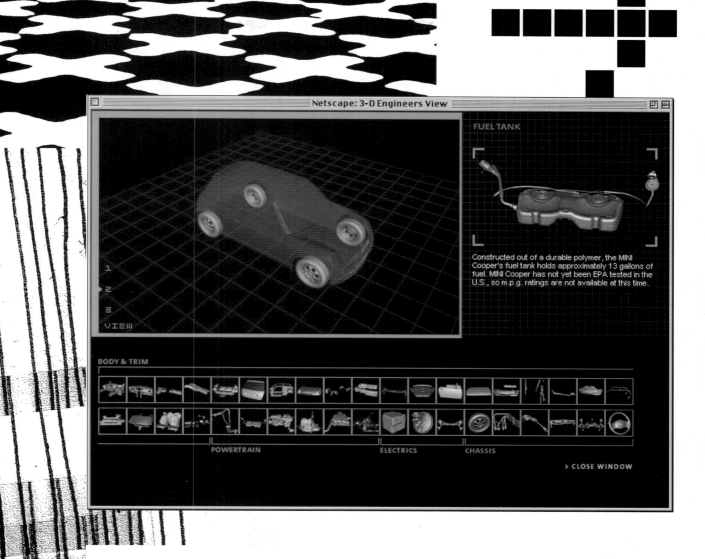

FUEL TANK

Constructed out of a durable polymer, the MINI Cooper's fuel tank holds approximately 13 gallons of fuel. MINI Cooper has not yet been EPA tested in the U.S., so m.p.g. ratings are not available at this time.

1
2
3
VIEW

BODY & TRIM

POWERTRAIN   ELECTRICS   CHASSIS

> CLOSE WINDOW

Cars and web design have quite a history. Nowadays, when automotive manufacturers want to build up anticipation for a new model, the web is an increasingly important part of their plans. The new Mini Cooper is no exception — indeed, the promotional site created to tell American consumers about it is one of the slickest yet. It is also a clear example of the benefits of web 3D. Visitors can look at spinnable 3D versions of the two new Mini Cooper models, as well as getting an engineer's view of their inner workings.

The 360-degree views section is certainly slick. In the right-hand window, a 3D model of the Mini Cooper appears. Move your mouse from left to right in the window, and it spins so that you can see it from every angle in the exterior view. The interior view is similar. But it's the 'Interior Tilt & Zoom' option that really impressed me the first time I saw it. It uses Quicktime, and lets you look around the interior of the car as if you really were sitting in the front seat. Of course, for real automotive nuts, it's no substitute for actually sitting in the vehicle, but it's certainly a start.

The site also has an 'Engineer's 3-D View' section, for the real automotive

360° VIEWS

MINI COOPER
> EXTERIOR
> **INTERIOR**
> INTERIOR
   WITH TILT & ZOOM
   (requires **Quicktime**)

MINI COOPER S
> EXTERIOR

SWITCH VIEW TO:
> MINI COOPER FEATURES & SPECS
> MINI COOPER S FEATURES & SPECS

minicooper_int_qtvr.mov

fanatics. It painstakingly explains the purpose of every single part of the new Mini, with technical specifications accompanied by pin-sharp 3D graphics to show how they fit into the whole car. There's a panel of the different parts at the bottom of the screen: click on one and you get a wireframe 3D image of the car, high-lighting where that part goes, as well as a close-up 3D image of the part itself.

What Mini USA proves for me is that certain areas — cars in particular — are ideally suited for web 3D. In fact, any website dealing with 3D products with an engineering focus is suited to 3D visualization, especially if there's an element of interactivity. It's not hard to think of potential ways that this technology can be taken further. Traditionally, car owners have relied on manuals and 2D diagrams to understand the way their vehicle works, and more importantly, how to fix faults. The Mini USA site shows how web 3D might be used to fulfil these functions more effectively online.

Macromedia was certainly impressed with the site's use of Flash — the company awarded it a Site of the Day award in January 2002. Meanwhile, the Mini Cooper has won plaudits from consumers and journalists alike. Its strong reputation in the US can at least be partially ascribed to the influence that the site has had. The great British car design has seduced American motorists once again, and ironically, the site itself was created by the UK arm of the Euro RSCG Circle agency.

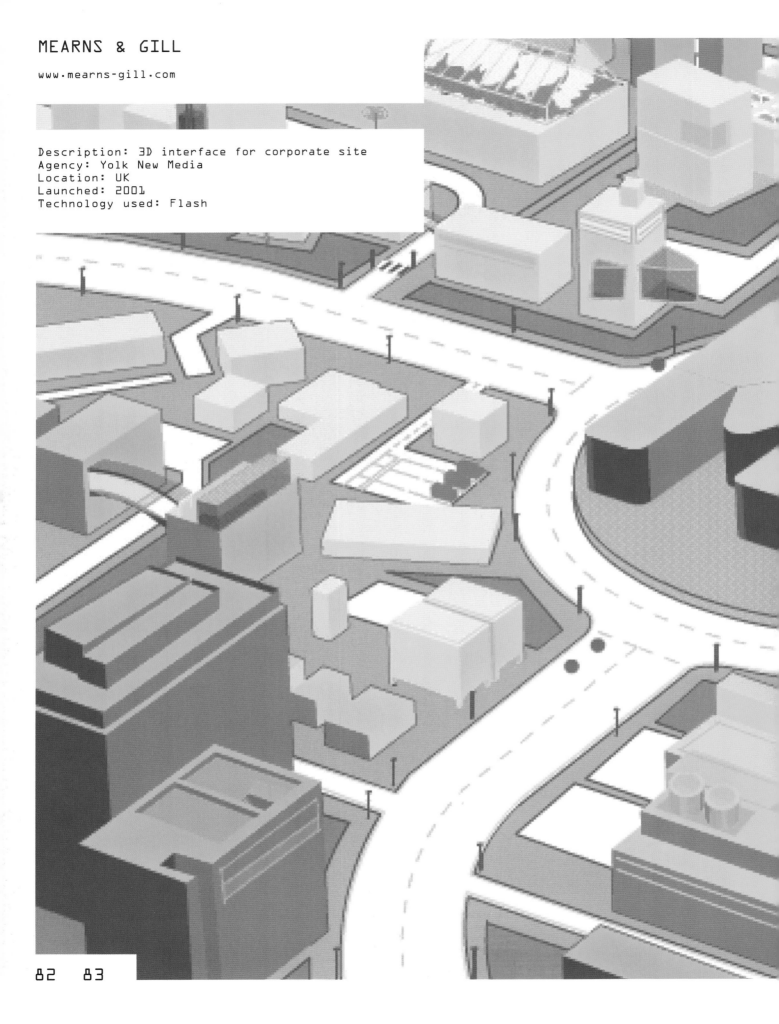

MEARNS & GILL

www.mearns-gill.com

Description: 3D interface for corporate site
Agency: Yolk New Media
Location: UK
Launched: 2001
Technology used: Flash

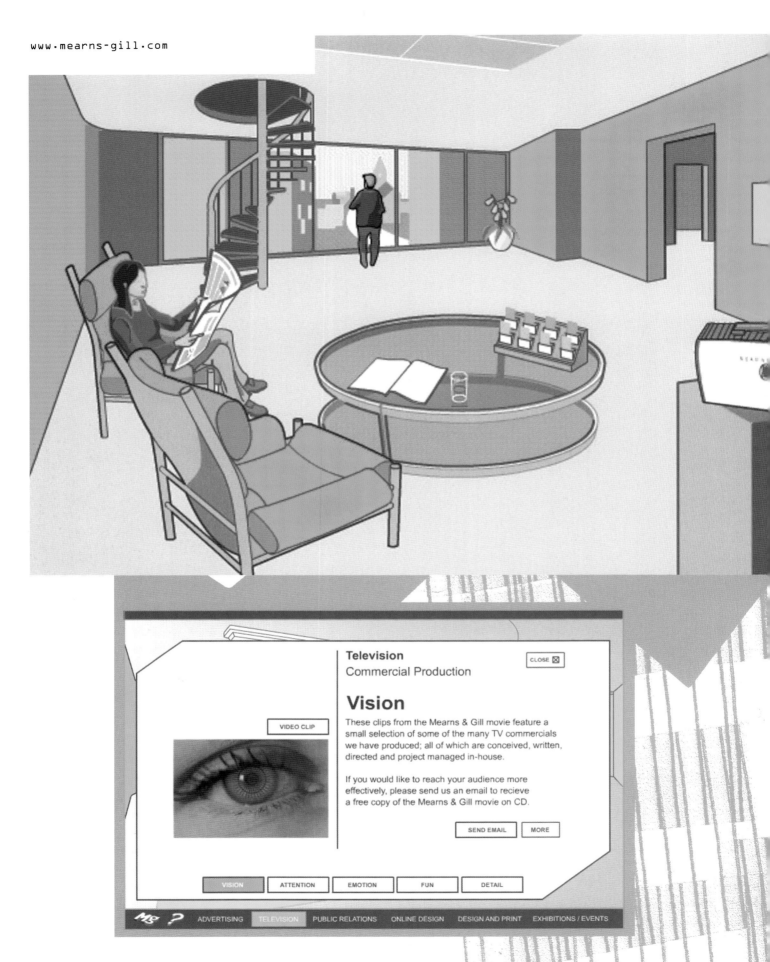

Television
Commercial Production

Vision

These clips from the Mearns & Gill movie feature a small selection of some of the many TV commercials we have produced; all of which are conceived, written, directed and project managed in-house.

If you would like to reach your audience more effectively, please send us an email to recieve a free copy of the Mearns & Gill movie on CD.

VIDEO CLIP

CLOSE ☒

SEND EMAIL   MORE

VISION   ATTENTION   EMOTION   FUN   DETAIL

Ms ?   ADVERTISING   TELEVISION   PUBLIC RELATIONS   ONLINE DESIGN   DESIGN AND PRINT   EXHIBITIONS / EVENTS

After the launch of Digit's MTV2 site in 2000, designers realized that you could craft an accessible, usable 3D interface to enable users to navigate around content that wasn't necessarily 3D. Of course, MTV2 was a site for a youth-oriented music TV channel, but there was no reason why a similar interface couldn't be applied to the corporate end of the market.

A number of agencies began experimenting with pseudo-3D interfaces, one of the most striking of which was Yolk New Media's site for Mearns & Gill, a communications consultancy based in Aberdeen, Scotland. Yolk is actually the in-house web team at the agency.

'This website is intended to be fun and informative', claims the blurb. 'We encourage you to roam with your cursor around the Mearns & Gill rooms; you never know what you might find!'

Roaming is the right word for it. The central hub of the site is an isometric cityscape, complete with buildings that pop up when you mouse over them, showing that they represent a section of the site. Clicking on them will then take you to that section, although you can also use the more conventional menu at the bottom of the screen.

Each section uses a similar pseudo-3D vector graphics look, forcing the user to move the cursor around the room to view examples of the company's work. This being the advertising industry, all of the above is naturally accompanied by a few bars of slick funk-jazz, looped endlessly. This being the web, there are also a few hidden extras, including a defiantly 2D Pong game.

If truth be told, the 3D navigation is more simplistic than MTV2, but it's effective and it doesn't get in the way of the content. There are millions of corporate sites on the web, many of which are staid and dull. Particularly in a creative industry such as advertising, there is considerable pressure on agencies to make their own sites fresh and vibrant, without throwing in loads of expensive bells and whistles that visitors will never want to use. In these latter cases web 3D can justly be accused of being self-indulgence on the part of designers.

The Mearns & Gill website, on the other hand, is what I'd describe as a good use of web 3D, and an example of how three-dimensional design doesn't have to break the rules of usability and effective web design. As more designers get used to Flash and related 3D technologies such as Swift 3D, I'd expect to see more of this kind of site appear. Advertising agencies are fairly open to these ideas, but interfaces like Mearns & Gill's may well bleed into more corporate sites for even larger businesses.

DUBIT

www.dubit.co.uk

Description: 3D chat environment
Agency: Lightmaker
Location: UK
Launched: 2001
Technology used: Flash, proprietary engine

Back when I was working on Cre@teonline magazine, we ran an issue themed around Flash, part of which was an extended feature on 'the world's top ten Flash designers'. A few weeks after the issue went on sale, I had a phone call from a designer at UK agency Lightmaker, demanding to know why they hadn't made the top ten. He wasn't seriously upset, of course — it was a cheeky attempt to get us to write about a new 3D chat site the agency was about to launch called Dubit. When we saw it, though, it was impressive enough not to need any strongarm tactics to make it into the magazine.

Dubit itself was a company set up by a group of teenagers who were fed up with not being able to buy things online, since they didn't qualify for credit cards. They came up with the idea of a 'Dubit' card, which would be a way for teenagers to make purchases online. Lightmaker was asked to come up with a community site to promote Dubit, so a chatroom seemed the obvious option.

The result was dubit.co.uk, with fifty separate environments, including a high street with cinema, bars, a games arcade, nightclubs and even a sex shop. It is presented in isometric 3D, looking not entirely dissimilar to Habbo Hotel. Visitors choose a character to walk around the site, and even get their own apartment to personalize. If truth be told, the characters are more 2D than 3D, but the environment is still impressive.

'We're a research and development house, but with the technologies we've developed, we can provide hardcore front-ends and back-ends', Lightmaker's Adrian Barrett told Cre@teonline, the month after the site's launch. 'You can't have a great front-end without a great back-end, so we built our own technology, EcommerceNewMedia, which we've developed over time. The proof of concept was already done when we came to the Dubit project, so we just had to build using it. 'It's a fully-functional, hardcore, dual-user Flash application server, and there isn't

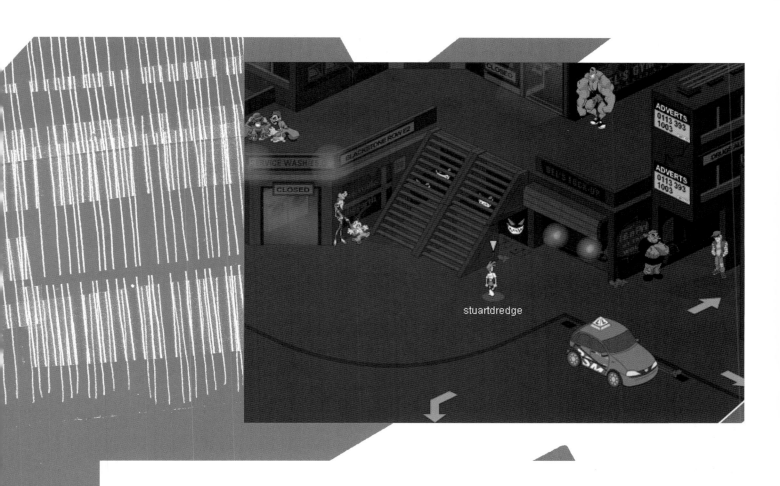

one available anywhere else. We've seen similar things in Shockwave, but we developed this in Flash because it's the most ubiquitous technology out there, and we wanted to keep file sizes to a minimum. For the environment you're getting, and the complexity of design, the file sizes are tiny.'

Visitors can choose a wide range of characters, including famous faces such as Snoopy, Eminem, various Star Wars characters and even Posh Spice and David Beckham. The result is a colourful environment full of crazy cartoon figures. Lightmaker's own corporate website uses the same technology, understandably, while the agency is busy looking for new applications for EcommerceNewMedia.

When Dubit was launched, Lightmaker had ambitions for transferring something like it to third-generation mobile phones. It remains to be seen whether that will be possible in the

near future, but it's heartening that they're ambitious enough to try. While many designers are getting excited about Shockwave 3D, the existence of chatrooms like Dubit shows that Flash can still offer a 3D trick or two of its own.

WILDTANGENT

www.wildtangent.com

Description: 3D gaming
Location: USA
Launched: 2000
Technology used: Proprietary Web Driver technology

0275

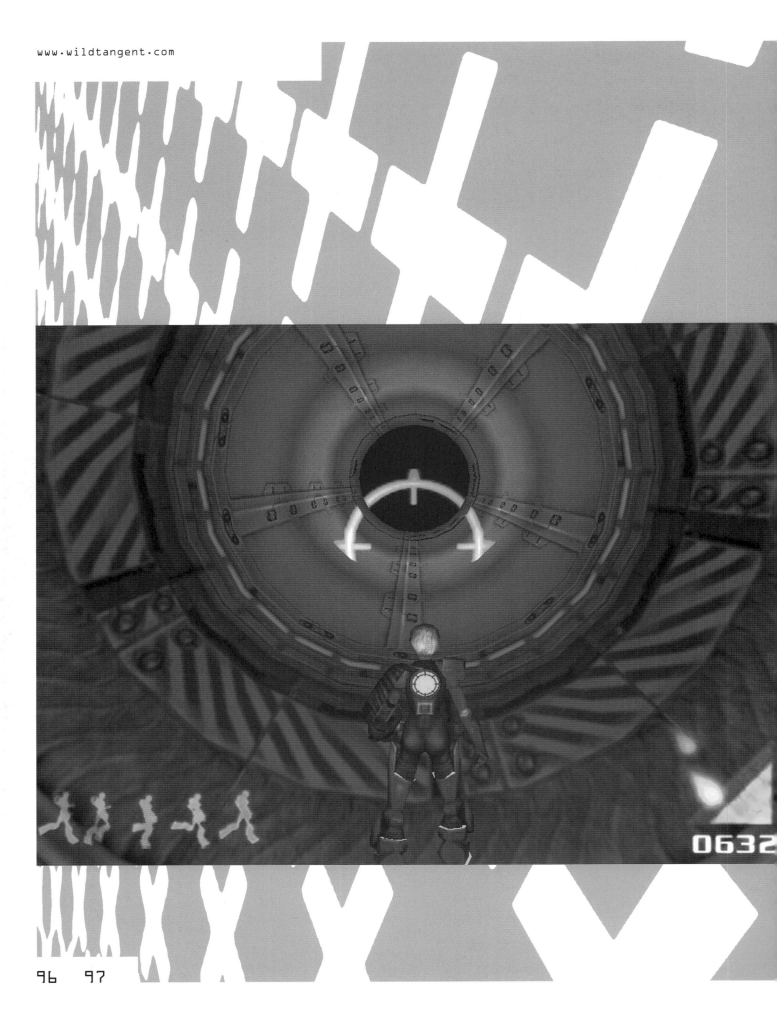

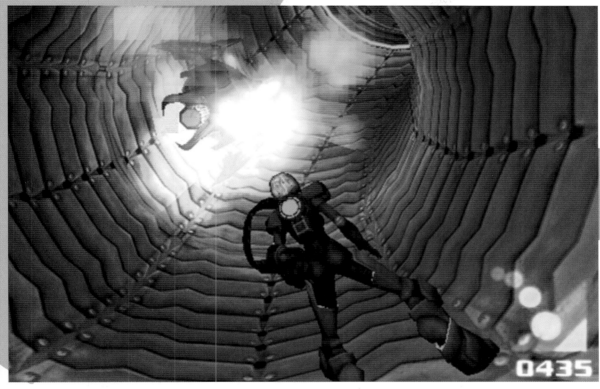
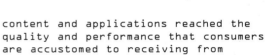

The move from 2D to 3D was revolutionary in the traditional games industry. It came with the debut of Sony's PlayStation, Sega's Saturn and Nintendo's N64 consoles, enabling developers to create truly immersive gaming worlds. The millions of gamers who have since bought Tomb Raider would presumably agree. Happily, web-based gaming is just entering the same stage. While Macromedia's Shockwave 3D technology has a large focus on the games market, it is also being boosted by third-party tools. WildTangent is a prime example.

The personalities behind WildTangent have strong credentials. President Alex St John previously worked at Microsoft, and was one of the creators of their DirectX technology. He was joined by Cambridge University scientist Jeremy Kenyon, who is Chief Technology Officer. To see the company's ambitious aims, check Alex's executive bio. 'The most popular multimedia technologies on the internet today have been obsolete in the consumer market for over six years', he says. 'It's time that web

content and applications reached the quality and performance that consumers are accustomed to receiving from titles delivered on CD-ROM.'

This puts the company into the same arena as 3D Groove, which can be seen elsewhere in this book. Take a look at the games that have been created using the firm's Web Driver technology, and you'll see it's a diverse range. One recent example is Invincible, an online game based on the film of the same name. It has users playing as two martial arts warriors, fighting against evil Shadowmen who are, as usual in this kind of game, trying to destroy all the good in the world. What's striking is the sheer quality of the graphics — like 3D Groove-powered games, they're more comparable to the visuals seen in recent console games.

Dark Orbit is another good example of WildTangent at work. Launched in October 2001 on Shockwave.com, it is an episodic sci-fi shoot-'em-up. Visitors can play the opening level for free, but must then pay $19.95 to play the rest of the game. It shows

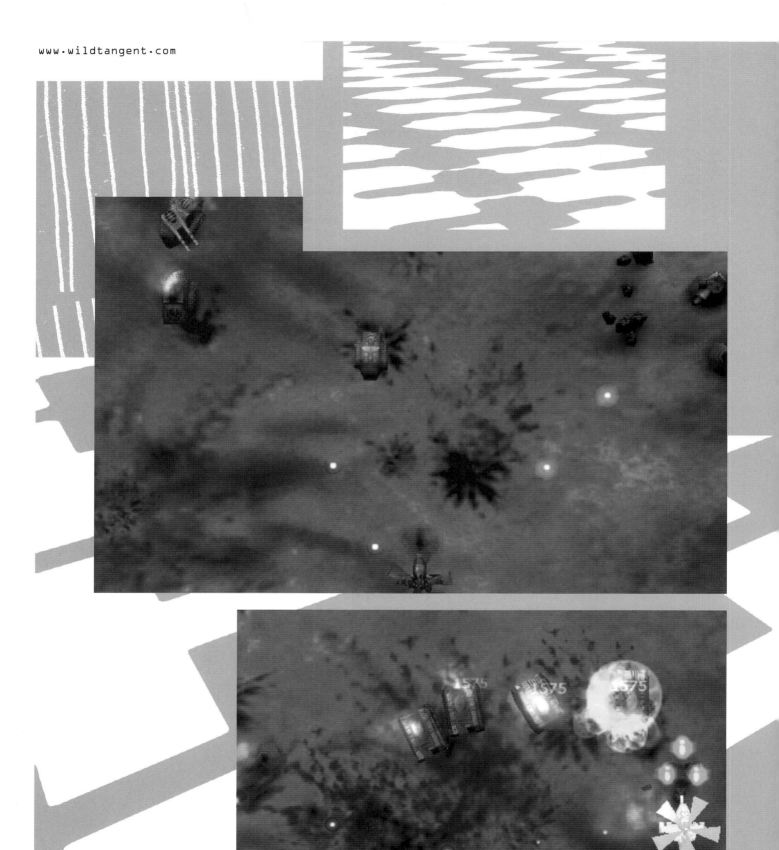

how web 3D is helping games sites like
Shockwave.com take the first steps
towards a pay model to help them stay
in business. Users generally aren't
prepared to pay for simple 2D Flash
games, but if they're getting almost
PlayStation-quality 3D visuals, they
might reach into their pockets.
Providing a free demo level harks back
to the days of shareware PC games like
Doom, which used a similar approach.

Dark Orbit is also noteworthy for
the fact that it was created by Phil
Shenk, who was previously the lead
artist on popular PC game Diablo II.
Technology such as Web Driver has the
potential to lure traditional games
developers onto the web. Games are
already one of the major areas for
web 3D, so with a continuing influx
of talent from traditional development
studios, they can only improve. What
I've noticed about WildTangent games
is that they're based very much on
the console model of quick-fix, high-
adrenaline arcade games, rather than
more lengthy strategic simulations.
This, I feel, should be the model
for future web 3D games.

UMA REAL ESTATE

www.concordebusinesspark.at

Description: 3D environment walkthroughs
Agency: Uma
Location: Austria
Launched: 2001
Technology used: VRML

The idea of online property walkthroughs isn't new: designers have been suggesting it since the earliest days of web 3D. Indeed, it was seen as one of the key potential uses for VRML. Yet, despite reports of intense interest from the real estate industry, it never quite took off. It was clear that people were prepared to research the house-buying process online, but it was thought that they simply weren't interested in walking through virtual representations of properties. However, there are currently a number of designers aiming to disprove this assumption. One is Austrian agency Uma, which is focusing on creating 3D walkthroughs for the commercial and business property market.

Concorde Business Park is the best example of Uma's 3D work. It's a 3D model of a Vienna-based business park, whose aim is to give potential buyers information about the location and advantages of being based there. The park itself hadn't been built when the site was launched, so visitors to the virtual landscape on the site could get a good idea of what it would eventually look like. Other similar sites include the Euro Plaza Office Park and the Innova Park, both created for an Innsbruck-based site.

Uma's founder, Christian Doegl, has been involved with web 3D since the earliest days of VRML, and he's been working in the area of online real estate for most of that time. He accepts that these kinds of 3D environments have not been successful in the past, but thinks that firms like Uma are now well placed to overcome the technical obstructions that remain.

'Users need to have a machine with a high enough processor,' he admits. 'Although that's not so much a problem as with streaming media. Also, broadband will make this kind of 3D work much more accessible to users. In Vienna, we already have quite a high number of broadband users, but elsewhere it's increasing too. Certainly, by the end of next year, the next-generation web will be coming through.'

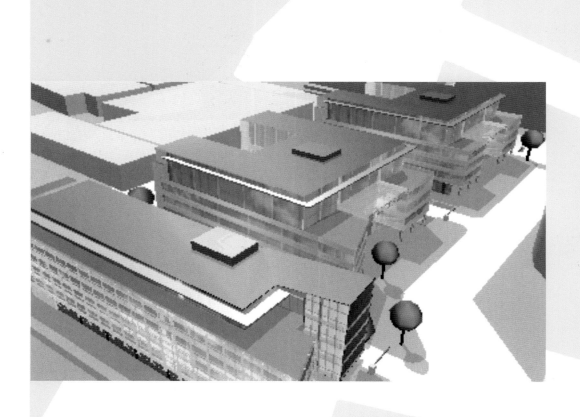

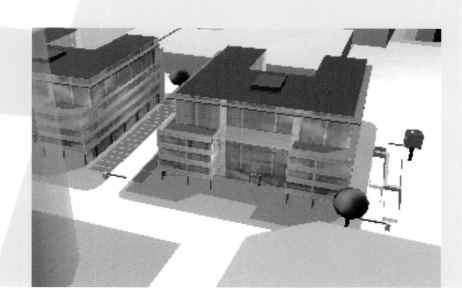

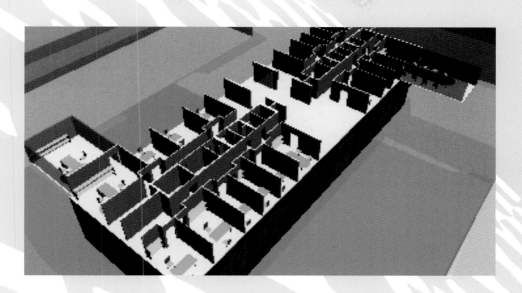

Among Uma's other 3D-related services is its knowledge-management division, which helps clients working in research fields to manage large amounts of data, and view it as 3D graphics. 'The aim is to provide very complex information in a very easy way', says Christian. 'We can describe in half a minute what would take thirty minutes to explain in other ways. We can visualize complex data taken from a database, so users don't have to scroll through fifty to a hundred pages of text.'

The firm also works on e-learning 3D environments for museums, cultural institutions and schools. This includes the development of a 3D multi-user engine to allow teachers to make presentations, and VICO (Virtual Interactive Collaboration Tool), which enables children to experiment and interact with new media in a virtual space. With all these different activities, Uma is one of the most interesting web 3D agencies in Europe. Earlier this year, the firm revamped its website to provide an English version. I'm fairly certain that a number of British and American web 3D designers will be keeping an eye on its content from now on.

RED PLAN-IT

www.hermanmillerred.com/planit

Description: 3D furniture configuration tool
Agency: Dots in Motion
Location: USA
Launched: 2001
Technology used: Viewpoint Experience Technology (VET)

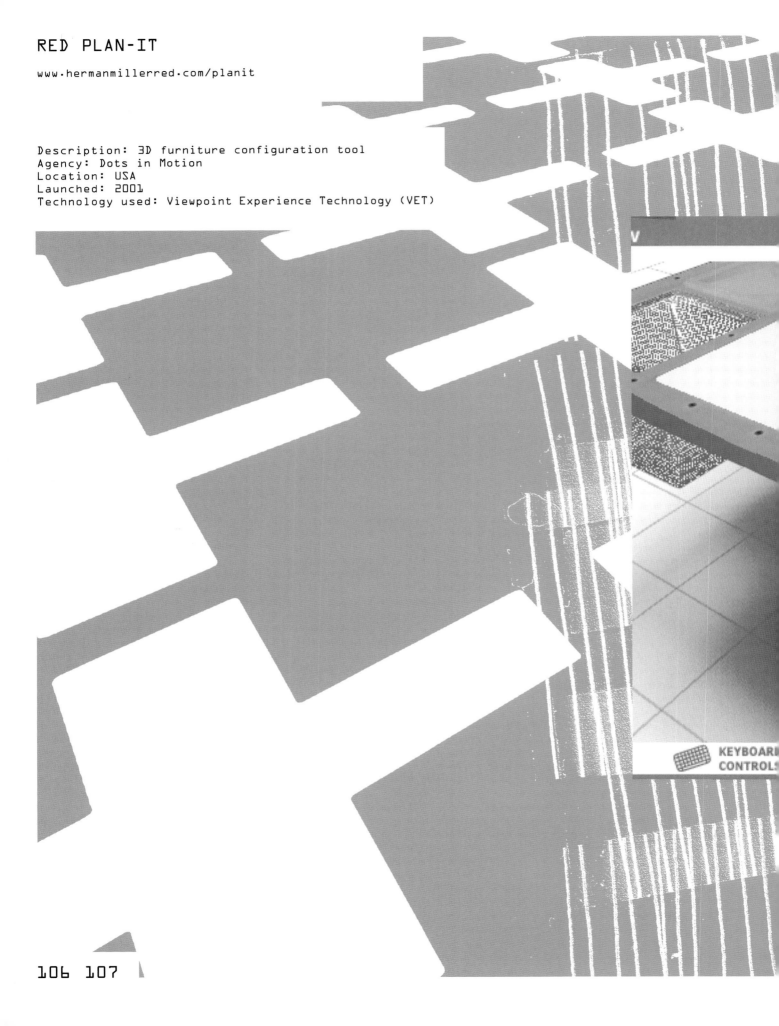

KEYBOARD
CONTROLS

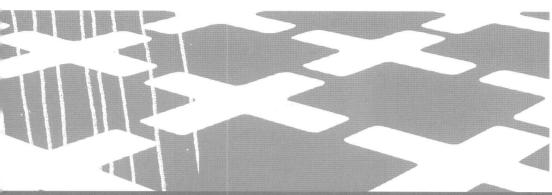

3D View Product List

Qty	Item	Price
1	ⓘ RED Snapper Desk Frame	$99.00
1	ⓘ RED Snapper Touch Pad	$25.00
2	ⓘ RED Snapper Storage Net	$30.00

4 Items	Total: $184.00

ADD TO CART	GO TO CHECKOUT

Location   **Info**

RED Snapper Storage Net

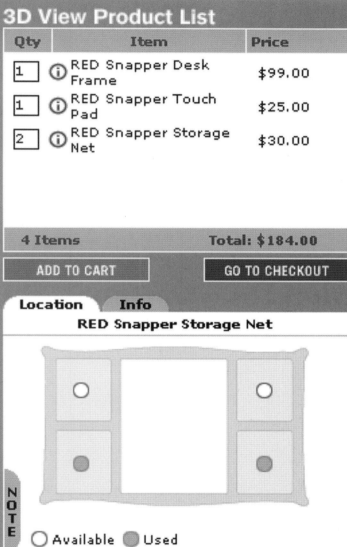

N
O
T
E

○ Available ● Used

ROTATE
ft click & drag

ZOOM
right click & drag

MOVE
both click & drag

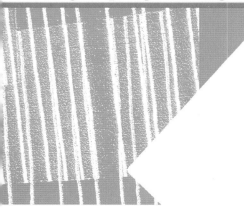

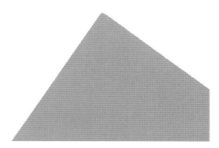

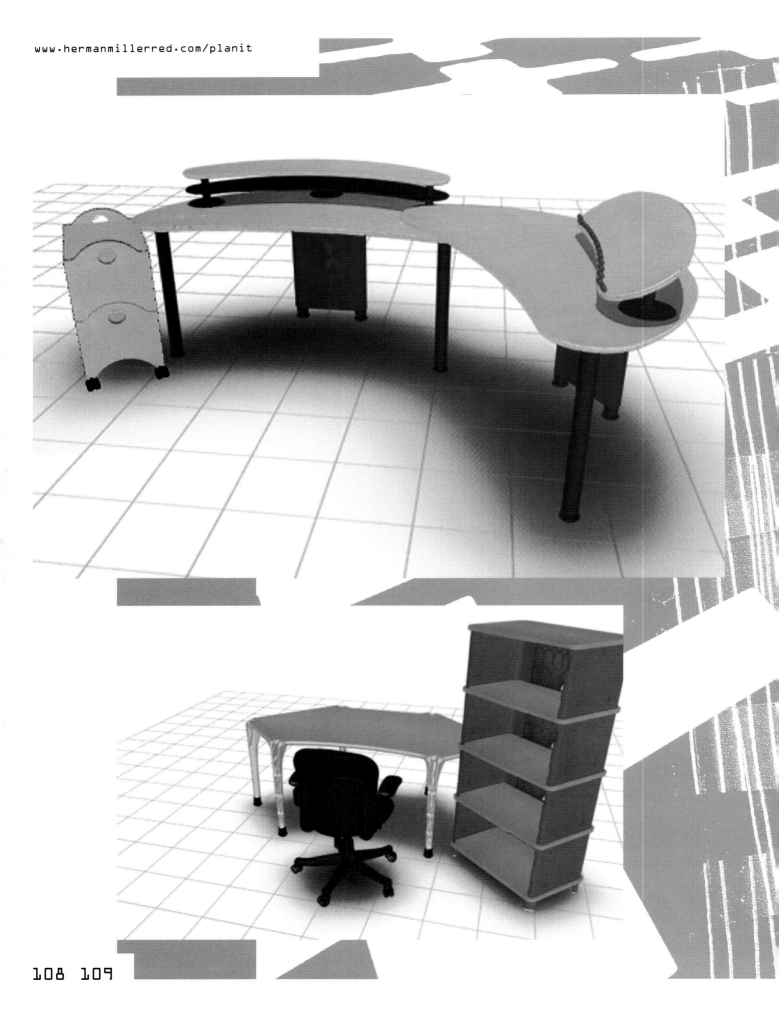

When it comes to ecommerce sites, web 3D has a chequered history. Just look at Boo.com for an example of an ambitious 3D scheme that ultimately didn't convince enough users to part with their cash to keep the site afloat. Yet 3D can still be a valuable tool for ecommerce sites. An increasing number of sites are using Viewpoint's visualization technology, one of the slickest being Herman Miller's RED Plan-It site.

Herman Miller is an interior design company that sells stylish furniture for offices and homes. RED Plan-It is a 3D configurator tool. It enables users to examine virtual 3D models of furniture from the firm's RED range, check out their prices and dimensions, fit them together into a custom-built workspace and then order the whole package with a single mouse click. It was developed by two US-based agencies: Dots in Motion from Michigan and Kanati from Texas, and was launched late in 2001. '3D doesn't simply add a wow factor any more', said Greg Clark, Herman Miller's brand manager for the RED range. 'This

technology truly melds form with function, and makes shopping online for complex products much easier.'

That, in a nutshell, is the point. Unlike some previous attempts at 3D ecommerce, RED Plan-It fulfils a clear need among visitors to the site — the desire to see how different bits of furniture look together — and has an extremely accessible interface to make it possible. Your 3D workstation is presented in the main viewing window, while below is a panel of extra products that you can add. So, for example, you might start with a base 'Rocket' desk, and opt to add a marker board, a phone stand or a trash bag (or, indeed, all three). Another window contains a basic top-down plan showing where you can put these extra products — click on an available slot, and the 3D scene changes immediately to show the results. You can then zoom in and out, or rotate the whole workstation around.

The advantage of using Viewpoint's technology is that the 3D models are high quality, but they don't take too

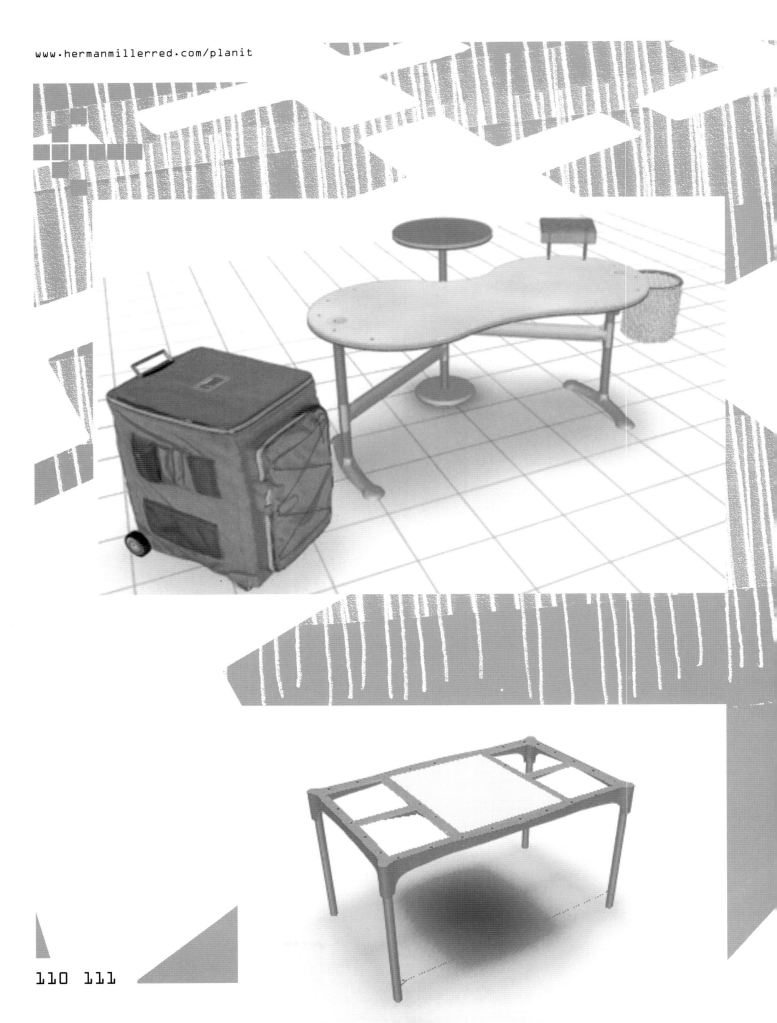

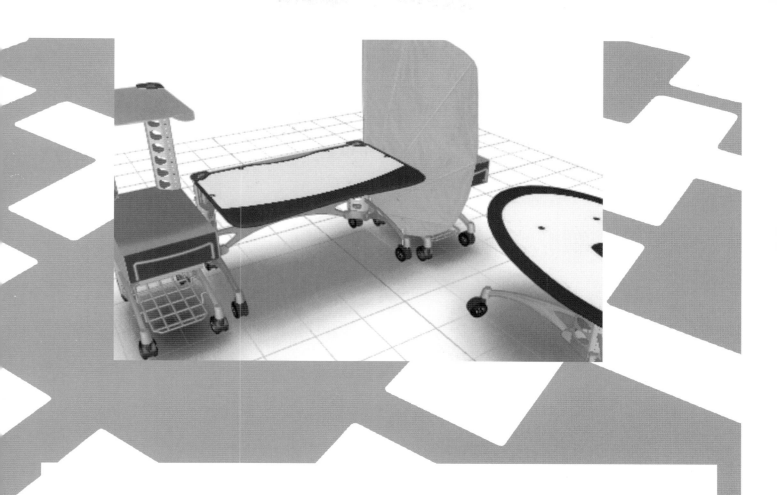

long to download. Even over a 56k
modem, RED Plan-It is perfectly usable.
Zooming, rotating and moving your
viewpoint can all be handled with
the mouse, too, making for a slick
interface. Most importantly, the 3D
elements are well integrated into the
rest of the site, so you can see items
appear in your shopping basket as you
add them to the 3D model. All in all,
it's one of the best examples of 3D
visualization ecommerce online.

There is, of course, a logical
continuation of this kind of modular
technology. It's great being able to
see how individual pieces of furniture
fit together, but it would be even
better to see how the finished result
would look in your own office or home.
Various technology companies are
working on this — Parallel Graphics
and INT3D for example — but it would
be surprising if Viewpoint doesn't
play an important part too. Sites like
RED Plan-It show that 3D visualization
can have a considerable impact on
ecommerce sites. Unfortunately, since
compiling this book, Herman Miller
have withdrawn the RED Plan-It range
and taken down the site.

SPACELOUNGE

www.it-quadrat.de/spacelounge/space.html

Description: Environment
Designer: Maik Ludewig
Location: Germany
Launched: 2000
Technology used: Adobe Atmosphere

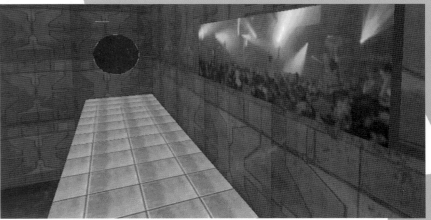

It's not every day that you get to play 3D noughts and crosses in a futuristic space station. In this one, the invisible computer opponent is particularly ruthless, racking up victory after victory. Maybe it's the cocktails you drank earlier in the virtual bar, or some subliminal effect caused by the ambient music pulsing away in the background.

This isn't the fantasy of a drug-addled sci-fi writer. This is SpaceLounge, an online world created by German designer Maik Ludewig, using the beta version of Adobe's Atmosphere. He launched it in April 2000, making it one of the first Atmosphere worlds to go live. 'It was intended as a testing and playing room for my first Atmosphere experiments', he says. 'I had the idea of a room somewhere in space, where you can listen to music, chat with your friends and see some of the effects that can be done with Atmosphere.'

Maik is such a big fan of Adobe's product that he's set up a companion website to SpaceLounge to serve the Atmosphere developer community. Having worked in the past with web 3D technologies like VRML, Java3D and Pulse, he's well qualified to judge the merits of Atmosphere. 'It was the combination of all the features I ever wanted to see in one web 3D tool', he says. 'It's got high-quality immersive virtual worlds, chat, avatars, custom animations and interactions, sounds and music, scripting and integration of high-detailed Viewpoint objects, which you can export from all major 3D modelling tools.'

Maik was particularly impressed by the inclusion of Javascript, which he has used a lot within SpaceWorld. 'Most web designers already know it, so they don't have to learn a new scripting language', he says. However, he thinks its biggest weakness so far is the lack of 3D hardware support for

Direct3D or OpenGL — although this is something that Adobe is currently trying to improve. When that happens, Maik plans to upgrade SpaceLounge to take full advantage. He has other ambitious plans, too.

'SpaceLounge will grow in size and beauty', he says. 'I will add more rooms and portals to my other worlds, which are in construction at the moment. It will be some kind of a portal room to my galaxy of worlds.' More generally, Maik thinks that web 3D will become 'trendy' again in 2002 and 2003. 'We'll see which application has the broadest install base, and so will dominate the market', he says. 'I think web 3D will then develop in a similar way to Flash, and will be a fixed part of the web in future.'

Meanwhile, he thinks that Atmosphere itself has potential for virtual ecommerce malls as well as online gaming and chat worlds. However, he also thinks it could be a big hit in the e-learning market. 'Imagine a virtual classroom, where the teacher shows interactive movies, and you can

whisper and talk to your classmates', he says. The sky's the limit, but Maik is keen to stress that the success or failure of web 3D will be down to the designers who work with it. 'How the web looks in five years time will depend entirely on our own creativity', he says.

VIRTUAL THEMEWORLD

www.virtualthemeworld.com

Description: Corporate branding site
Agency: Digital Arts
Location: UK
Launched: 2001
Technology used: Director 8.5

BEYOND LIMITS ZONE

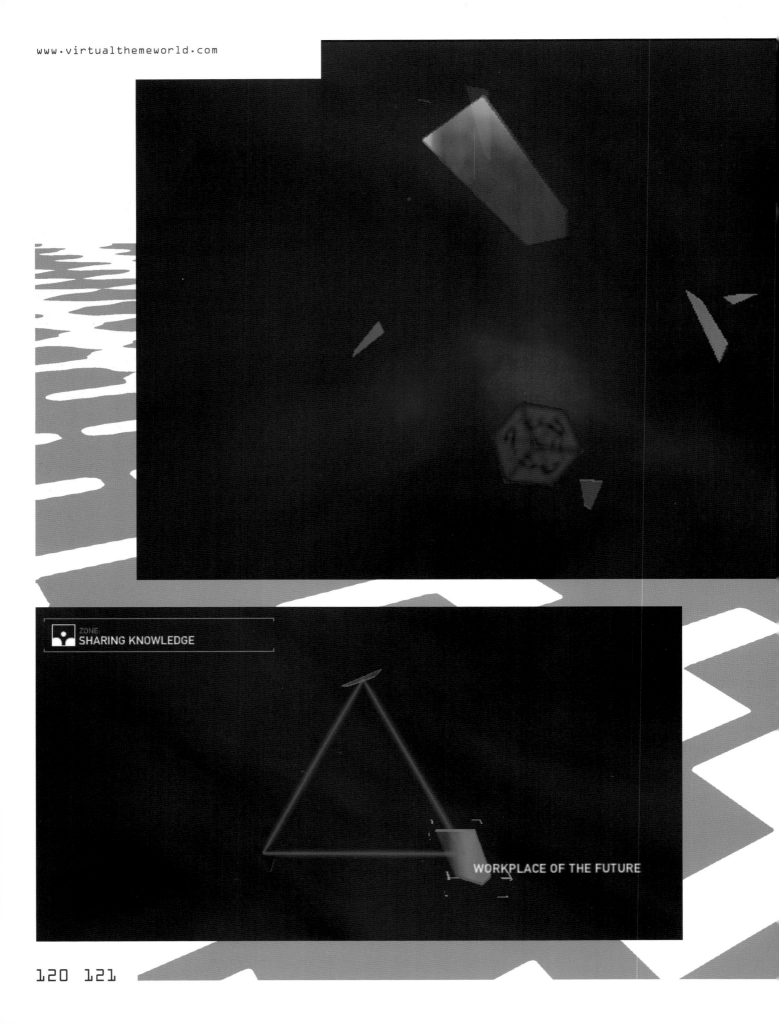

ZONE:
SHARING KNOWLEDGE

WORKPLACE OF THE FUTURE

ZONE
CITIZENSHIP

MENU
TEXT
VIDEO
LINKS

TEXT
THE TRADITIONAL COMMUNITY
The term 'community' - from the Latin communis, meaning common - conveys a sense of fellowship, sharing and altruism. It implies membership of an interest group with shared experiences. The German philosopher Tonnies made the first distinctions between community and society. He defined community as the expression of natural will, characterized by solidarity, kinship and custom. Society, on the other hand, results from rational will and exists for clearly defined purposes. A family or clan is a community. Armies and companies are social entities. Definitions of community through the 20th century included geographical, social and historical parameters.
PAGES
◄ 1 2 3 4 ►

VIRTUAL COMMUNITIES

Web 3D has made little impact on corporate websites, especially when it comes to their user interfaces. Most corporate sites have clung onto their flat 2D menus, and rightfully so, given that visitors are generally just looking for fast access to information. This leaves no place for experimental 3D navigation. Occasionally, however, businesses commission pure branding websites that require something more adventurous. A good example is Virtual Themeworld.

The site was created for Swiss Re by the London agency Digital Arts, which has since closed its doors. The site describes itself as 'an interactive multimedia environment which presents and expresses ideas in a myriad of forms about the world of risk'. This high-brow concept required an equally challenging user interface to lift it above the crowd. Former Digital Arts designer Matt Bindoff explained the thinking behind it. 'We wanted to buck the trend of the usual website point-and-click paradigm. We envisioned a seemingly infinite immersive environment, so 3D was the obvious choice. It's not 3D for the sake of 3D, though. It added the sensation needed to immerse the user.'

There were some constraints to work within, naturally. Swiss Re stressed that no non-standard browser plug-ins could be used, so Digital Arts opted for Shockwave instead. The first version of Virtual Themeworld was produced using Director 8, in combination with the agency's own proprietary 3D engine. 'It was quite rudimentary,' says Matt. 'It was capable of pushing about 80 quad polys at 15 frames-per-second on a G3.'

At this point, Digital Arts started working on a second version, which would have an improved engine and a revamped interface. This coincided with Macromedia's release of Director

? TO FLY CLICK AND HOLD DOWN THE MOUSE. MOVE THE
MOUSE TO CHANGE DIRECTION...

8.5, complete with its new 3D functionality and hardware renderer. 'The
demos we achieved in a couple of days
blew both us and the client away',
remembers Matt. Progress was quick
from this point onwards. The 3D models
were coded and given textures created
in Photoshop, while Digital Arts'
programming team build a content-
management system. This used Shockwave
as its front-end, talking to a MySQL
database via PHP for the back-end.

The Virtual Themeworld site was
intended to be a grand project, but
since its launch, the content hasn't
been updated as often as was originally
expected. Nevertheless, its importance
— and the reason for including it in
this book — is the example it presents
to other businesses who don't think
web 3D has anything to offer their
online projects.

Matt talks candidly about the skills
which programmers need to produce this
kind of 3D content. 'Any coders without
3D maths experience will find producing
any complex interaction in 3D pretty
difficult', he says. 'A good knowledge
of A-level Maths is a definite
advantage. The maths for Virtual

Themeworld was simple enough, but the
major hurdle was the inability to
display sprites over the Shockwave 3D
environment.'

Matt is somewhat gloomy about the
current uses for 3D navigation on the
web. 'Most 3D interfaces I've come
across online are highly-convoluted,
annoying systems', he says, claiming
that Virtual Themeworld's random
nature makes it an exception. However,
he does have some ideas for 3D content
on other sites. 'I'd like to see 3D
representations of property on estate
agents' sites, more to give a feeling
of size and space rather than visual
accuracy. If you could then import
your furniture and see how well it
fitted, it would be cool.'

ZONE
BEYOND LIMITS

MENU
TEXT
VIDEO

TEXT
Original Design Brief

Swiss Re chose Digital Arts to design and create the Virtual Themeworld - a next generation platform from which they could showcase events and topics to be explored at the Centre for Global Dialogue in Ruschlikon.

Digital Arts aimed to realise concepts using technology and visuals to create a truly immersive user experience for both the internet and on-site version called the Command Room. In order to achieve the effect of flying, Digital Arts created a 3D environment using open GL and Direct X application for use within the Command Room version and due to the limitations of

PAGES
◀ 1 2 3 4 ▶

THE MAKING OF THE VIRTUAL THEMEWORLD

B3D MUSIC VIDEOS

www.brilliantdigital.com/solutions/music

Description: Animated 3D web music clips
Agency: Brilliant Digital
Location: Australia
Launched: 2001
Technology used: b3d Studio

The music industry hasn't always been quick to catch on to the web's benefits — witness the ongoing saga of Napster and other file-swapping services. Yet there is one area where record companies have been keen to make the most of cutting-edge web technologies, and that's 3D web videos, courtesy of a technology developed by Australian firm Brilliant Digital. Its b3d Studio software enables designers to create 3D animated videos for bands or singers, often with an interactive game element. Artists to have benefited from the b3d treatment so far include Sum 41, Ja Rule, DMX and Sisqo. The idea is simple — users watch the videos, or even play them if there are game-like elements. All the while, they're hearing the artist's latest single or album tracks. Users view the content through Brilliant Digital's proprietary b3d Projector player. The results are extremely visually impressive, although you really need a broadband connection and a relatively recent 3D graphics card in your computer to make the most of them.

Late in 2001, the company signed a deal to include the Projector software with the software needed for the Morpheus and KaZaA file-sharing services — two of the most popular tools that people use to swap MP3 music files. Thanks to this, b3d Projector has become one of the most downloaded 3D players on the web, with more than 40 million users at the time of writing — even if most of them won't know they've got it until they encounter content like the web music videos.

Much of the existing b3d music content is based around hip-hop artists, particularly on the popular Def Jam label. In August 2001, Brilliant Digital even appointed Def Jam supremo Russell Simmons to its board of directors, forging a close link. 'People expect entertainment on the internet to be even more fresh and exciting than traditional platforms', he said at the time. 'These animated web music videos use the internet to bring the same type of innovation that MTV provided consumers with during the early eighties with the launch of music videos.'

The b3d music videos offer an intriguing
glimpse into how web 3D can be used
to provide a middle ground between the
big-budget music videos that are shown
on MTV and the kind of 3D games that
people play on consoles like Xbox or
PlayStation2. It's that blend of motion
and interactivity, and what's more it
makes best use of the interactivity
that users expect when they're surfing
the web. With millions of music fans
already using the b3d player, courtesy
of Morpheus or KaZaA, the future for
this technology looks bright.

Hybrid music videos/games could have
a huge impact on online promotions.
Record companies are already
experimenting with simple 2D games
to promote their acts, but it remains
to be seen whether they'll be brave
enough to commission more ambitious
content, like the b3d videos. Either
way, the work being carried out by
Brilliant Digital offers a glimpse
into the future. Meanwhile, the firm
is investigating other areas — its
Studio and Projector technologies can
also be used for banner advertising,
web animation, 'edutainment' and sport.

DESIGN ASSEMBLY

www.designassembly.de

Description: 3D games engine
Agency: Design Assembly
Location: Germany
Launched: 2001
Technology used: Flash

TIME 0:23:44

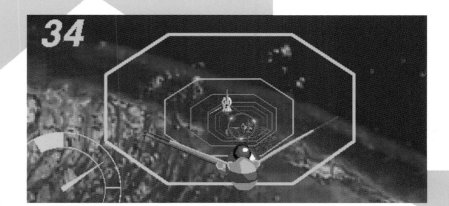

There has been plenty of hype surrounding the 3D capabilities of Macromedia's Shockwave platform, but a number of web designers are continuing to explore the potential of its sibling, Flash. One such designer is Thomas Wagner, of German agency Design Assembly. Although the firm creates 3D Flash games for a range of clients, it has also coded its own proprietary engine for the task.

'Unfortunately, most people still think that Flash games have to be simple drag'n'drop or point'n'click puzzles', says Thomas Wagner. 'But when Flash 4 came out, I was convinced that we could use it to give classic 16-bit arcade games from the SNES, Amiga and Atari ST some kind of renaissance on the web.'

Thomas quickly put his thoughts into practice, writing some simple jump'n'run games. There were problems though — not least of which was the fact that Flash 4 didn't have any collision detection. Wagner busied himself with working out ways to control many objects, yet still keeping the frame rate at a healthy 40 frames-per-second.

'Once you do this in a 2D space, it's no problem to render all the objects in 3D. Flash has the great advantage that your codings don't have to care about things like scaling or even loading bitmaps, so you can easily realize even those games that would never have been possible on 16-bit machines, like Space Harrier, After Burner or Out Run.'

The upshot of all this was Design Assembly's 3D Flash gaming engine, which it then licensed to web-design agencies who were creating games for their clients. For example, London agency Design.net created a 3D fighter-jet game for a recruitment site for the British Royal Air Force. However, Design Assembly has since taken its technology back in-house. 'There are still so many oddities with Flash that you must have at least some experience when dealing with it', he explains. 'It would be sad if people use my coding to make a game that doesn't run fast enough or look nice. The coding is important, sure, but not as important as good gameplay and visual appearance.'

PLAYER 1 best

lap 1

ap 0:0

SCORE 7300

Thomas cites the example of designers using too large transparent GIF graphics as one common mistake that can slow even the best game engine down. 'There are many tricks and hints that I can give. Normally, you need them all to make a good game, and a good game is the best advertising for us, so I feel happier when I can do it for myself.'

He doesn't think that Flash's 3D capabilities will be significantly improved in the near future, considering Macromedia's positioning of Director as its flagship 3D product. Nevertheless, there are certain changes he would like to see implemented in Flash — for example, the addition of calculation functions which would make it easier to render 3D positions on a 2D display. 'The most important thing would be a completely new render engine. At the moment, there's no hardware support, even though you could easily use DirectX without making the Flash player any bigger. At the moment, if you switch Flash to full screen, it slows down too much. It's a shame.'

For the moment, Design Assembly is continuing to work as a general design agency, but Thomas hopes eventually to specialize in the gaming side, both online and off. It is clear that the firm's Flash engines will continue to be useful. 'I don't think that our main business will be selling the engines,' he says. 'But it's nice for our customers to know that we have them ready, and can easily build a customized game for them.'

ASIMO 3D

www.honda.co.jp/ASIMO/controller/enjoy_01p3.html

Description: 3D product visualization of robot
Location: Japan
Launched: 2001
Technology used: Viewpoint Experience Technology

3DのASIMOを操作しよう！
ASIMOコントローラー。

ボタンを押すと、3DのASIMOが動きます

HOW TO PLAY

 回転
Click & Drag

 ズーム
Ctrl + Click & Drag

 移動
Shift + Click & Drag

ASIMOと遊ぼう！

3DのASIMOを操作しよう！
ASIMOコントローラー。

ASIMO

ボタンを押すと、3DのASIMOが動きます

3D
HOW TO PLAY

 回転
Click & Drag

 ズーム
Ctrl + Click & Drag

 移動
Shift + Click & Drag

ASIMOと遊ぼう！

3DのP3を
360°見てみよう！

Hu... P3

HOW TO PLAY

回転
Click & Drag

ズーム
Ctrl + Click & Drag

移動
Shift + Click & Drag

Japanese creatives have been responsible, through the years, for some of the world's most visually arresting 2D design, whether it be artwork, animation or video games. The country has a well-deserved reputation for its 2D work, yet there is also a burgeoning web 3D community. Take a look, for example, at www.digikoku.com, which is a resource site for creatives using the Cult 3D tool.

Viewpoint, too, has seen a number of designers take up its visualization technology. In December 2001, it signed a distribution agreement with Kubota Graphics Technologies (KGT), a firm that specializes in digital visualization for medical, scientific, engineering and educational applications. Even before this deal, Viewpoint had attracted some large corporations, including Subaru and Honda. The latter has used Viewpoint technology to showcase a number of its vehicles, as well as Asimo, its humanoid entertainment robot.

Unfortunately, the first thing you notice is the obtrusive Viewpoint branding plastered over the viewing window, which gets in the way of you and the 3D model of Asimo. Still, it's a good thing the model itself is so personable. You can spin Asimo round, zoom in and out to take a closer look, and move it around the viewing window. This is fun enough, but there's more to it than mere movement.

By clicking on one of the six action buttons below the viewing window, you can watch the virtual Asimo perform a number of actions with all the smoothness of his real-world incarnation. He bows, he walks towards you and back again, he waves, shakes hands, gesticulates and even executes a nifty shuffle on demand. This can all be viewed from any angle, using Viewpoint's simple mouse-dragging interface.

Irritating corporate branding aside, the Asimo site is impressive because it demonstrates an application for web

ASIMOと遊ぼう！

3DのP3を
360°見てみよう！

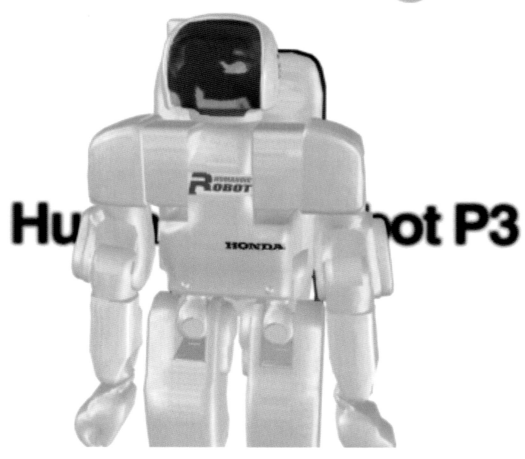

Hu **ot P3**

3D
HOW TO PLAY

 回転
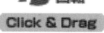
Click & Drag

ズーム
Ctrl + Click & Drag

 移動
Shift + Click & Drag

3DのP3を
360°見てみよう！

Humanoi P3

HOW TO PLAY

回転
Click & Drag

ズーム
Ctrl + Click & Drag

移動
Shift + Click & Drag

3D that genuinely adds value. Honda's robot is amazingly impressive when you see it moving in real life, but in grainy web video you don't get the same sense of its smooth motion. Web 3D is a happy compromise, getting across the vital sense of its seamless motion. Of course, it also helps that Asimo isn't being reduced to a mere 2D animation.

It's true that this site in its current incarnation is somewhat limited — the attraction of spinning and zooming in on a robot does wear off after a while. But it is a good demonstration of how web 3D can be used to explain new technologies, from robots through to consumer electronics devices and cars.

Strangely, the growth of the web itself has been fairly slow in Japan, although more people now have access to an internet connection. As larger number of Japanese consumers get online, I'd expect more web 3D content to appear, in even more sophisticated incarnations. There's a talented community of 3D designers emerging, making use of a number of different 3D technologies. It'll be particularly fascinating if creatives start focusing their energies on bringing Japanese animation culture to the web in a 3D form.

CONCLUSION

Conc-lus-ion

The sheer variety of content showcased in this book demonstrates that 3D technologies are already playing an important part on the web. In some areas, this is still at the experimental stage, but in others, designers are using them right now for client-based commercial work. Either way, it's clear that they're getting under way with a new determination.

Web 3D is much better positioned for success than it was five years ago, for a number of reasons. Firstly, there are better tools available. Adobe and Macromedia have entered the market with the dedicated web 3D products, Atmosphere and Director 8.5. Meanwhile, high-end offline packages such as Maya, Softimage, 3ds Max and Lightwave all have options to export content for use online.

Secondly, web designers have more knowledge and experience now. Many of the creatives who cut their teeth on VRML are still coming up with ambitious ideas, but they have five years more experience of how to successfully implement them. What's more, they've been joined by a new generation of talented web designers — people who have grown up with 3D content on their games consoles. As an industry, we also have more experience of how users interact with online content of all kinds, which can only help.

These are promising signs, but they only provide potential. To realize it, designers need to be pragmatic about what kinds of 3D content can be successful online. Experimental work aside, whenever designers are tempted to use web 3D, they should be sure that it is demonstrably more effective than the 2D alternative. With this in mind, there are a number of areas where I believe it will be important in the coming years.

ONLINE GAMES

You don't need a crystal ball to predict the success of online 3D games; it's already happening today. The release of Director 8.5 in 2001 kicked off a new wave of three-dimensional game development, which had already been bolstered by dedicated tools from firms such as the Groove Alliance and WildTangent. Already bored of creating simple 2D Flash rip-offs of Breakout and Space Invaders, designers were eager to investigate the potential for 3D.

We have the existing model of console games to show us that the move from two to three dimensions is a natural one. Just trace the route from Pong through to isometric 8-bit games like Head Over Heels, and onto fully immersive 3D games such as Tomb Raider and Quake. There's no reason why web games shouldn't follow the same path, particularly when firms like the Groove Alliance are boasting that their latest technology is up to PlayStation-quality visuals.

Designers will continue to stretch development software as far as it will go — and further — in order to emulate the most successful offline games. These technologies must continue to improve to keep up with their ambitions. There's also the bandwidth question. As more internet users get high-speed connections, so designers will have more freedom to create rich 3D gaming environments.

Above all, designers creating 3D games for the web need to keep in mind the medium's strengths, and the specific needs of its audience. It is foolish simply to attempt to mimic console games, since the web is far outstripped by next-generation machines such as PlayStation2, Xbox and Gamecube. If people want to play an involving 3D action adventure, they'll turn to their console.

Web games — whether 2D or 3D — need to be simple, instantly accessible and playable in short bursts — ideally against other people around the world. As long as web designers bear this in mind, they'll be sure to find healthy audiences for their work. It is also clear that there is going to be a big market for 3D promotional games created for corporate clients. Creative agencies will be using simple projects like these to learn the skills that will help them create their own 3D gaming content later on.

CHAT ENVIRONMENTS

Web users aren't simply interested in shooting each other or playing golf; sometimes they just want to socialize. The internet has a rich history of chat applications, from the text-based world of IRC and MUDS through to the more visual 2D environments, where users are represented on-screen by cartoon avatars. The move into 3D was always likely to happen, albeit with varying degrees of success.

Currently, there are two kinds of 3D chat environment. There are the isometric communities such as Habbo Hotel and Dubit, which use pixelly graphics akin to 8-bit games from the 1980s, and three-dimensional versions of the cartoon characters seen in 2D chatrooms. People are using Flash or, increasingly, Shockwave to create these kinds of sites. Then there's the full-3D chat environments, using an interface more similar to modern games like Quake or Phantasy Star Online. Although these kinds of chatsites were pioneered using VRML, the release of Adobe's Atmosphere has given them a boost. So how are both types set up for success in the future?

The isometric 3D chat-sites are well-placed, especially when they're supported by a solid back-end engine, as in the cases of Habbo Hotel and Dubit. The visual style of these

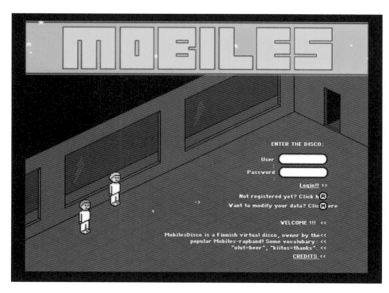

environments particularly appeals to twentysomethings who grew up with the computer games that inspired it. Mobiles Disco, the foreunner to Habbo, became a busy haunt for new media creatives, for example.

In my opinion, the future of fully 3D chatrooms is less assured, at least when chat is the sole purpose. While hanging out in various Atmosphere worlds as part of the research for this book, I often found myself standing in a circle with three or four other users, paying no attention to the surrounding scenery. It does make you wonder why you should waste your processing power on scenery that you're not going to notice. It's no surprise that Adobe isn't pitching Atmosphere as a pure 3D-chatroom tool.

An important element in the future of 3D chat environments of both kinds will be avatar-customization. One of the advantages of 3D chat is that it enables you to create a richer visual representation of yourself — realistic or otherwise. A glimpse of the future can be seen in the work of companies such as US-based Digitalspace, whose Traveller technology offers voice-activated avatars. You speak into your PC microphone, and on-screen your avatar's lips move as other users hear your words come out of their speakers. Sound may well be the next revolution in 3D chat environments.

I've got one concern about 3D chat environments, though — they tend to re-impose the spatial constraints of the real world. In a text-based chatroom, the conversation ebbs and flows as a stream of thoughts, rants, questions and views. You can dive in with your own opinions, or simply lurk in the background and watch the text flow. In a 3D chatroom, however, you've got a physical presence there on screen. The first time I logged on to Habbo Hotel, the lobby was dotted with clumps of people seemingly deep in conversation. Breaking into these chats is as intimidating as walking into a real-world party where you don't know anyone. It's hard to think of a way to solve this problem, aside from suggesting that users who don't like it will naturally gravitate towards old-school text chatrooms.

ECOMMERCE

Here's a notion about how web 3D could revolutionize ecommerce. One day, we'll be able to stroll our virtual avatar through the aisles of a virtual supermarket, picking up virtual items and putting them into our virtual shopping basket. Then, we'll walk next door to browse the virtual shelves of Amazon, before trying on clothes in the virtual Marks & Spencer. Will this ever happen? Put it this way: I'm virtually certain it won't.

The best thing about the web is that it frees us from these real-world constraints. Usability guru Jakob Nielsen put it well back in 1998 with his '2D is Better than 3D' Alertbox column. 'The goal of web design is to be better than reality', he wrote. 'If you ask users to "walk around the mall", you are putting your interface in the way of their goal.'

Does this mean that web 3D will have no impact on ecommerce in the future? No. 3D visualization has considerable potential. Businesses such as Nike, Compaq and Herman Miller are already using Viewpoint's technology, and more are sure to follow. The key thing to bear in mind is that 3D visualization works well for certain products, but not for others. Trainers and furniture fall into the former category, while books and CDs clearly fall into the latter.

Clothing is a trickier proposition. The failure of Boo.com seemed to prove that users weren't more likely to part with their cash if they could see how garments looked on 3D virtual mannequins. That said, the technology

was brand new and rather heavy going — when Boo folded, its design team was working on a sleeker version using dHTML rather than Flash.

Boo.com used standard mannequins, but when considering the potential for 3D ecommerce, the possibilities for avatars are intriguing. Imagine if every user had an avatar stored on their computer that was accurately modelled on their own dimensions, they could 'try on' clothes to get a good idea of how they'd look in them. The necessary technologies are currently in development, and it will be interesting to see which retailer is willing to take the gamble.

Visualization isn't just about spinning 3D models of individual objects. A number of firms are working on technologies that enable users to see how certain pieces of furniture — chairs, tables, cupboards, etc — would fit into their home or office space. Call it environment visualization, if you like. This is one of the possible uses for Atmosphere, but there are also dedicated technologies in existence.

In June 2001, for example, Parallel Graphics launched Outline 3D, an interior design application aimed at furniture retailers, manufacturers and home and garden portals. Users can create and decorate a 3D room, before dragging and dropping products into it. 'Customers can now see how potential purchases will look, and get a genuine feel for the room and furniture before they buy', explains marketing manager Gavin Divilly.

Taking this a step further, there is also much potential for 3D walkthroughs, particularly in the real-estate market. Few people would buy a house based purely on a virtual walkthrough on an estage agent's website, but it might help them decide whether a property is worth viewing. Once again, though, while web designers

Digimask Viewer- C:\My Documents\Stuar...

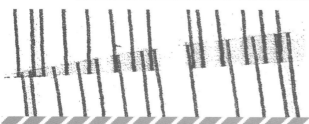

will be keen to implement this kind of technology in the future, they will have to convince their clients that it's worthwhile.

E-LEARNING

Games, chatrooms and ecommerce are the three biggest applications for web 3D in the future, but there's a fourth, e-learning, which is the dark horse of the bunch. It can be broken down into two areas: educational sites aimed at children and students, or online content created by businesses to train their staff remotely.

An example of the former is Parallel Graphics' 3D periodic table, created in 2000 to showcase the firm's technology. When trying to illustrate complex molecular structures, 3D graphics have a clear advantage. In the next few years, web designers will be looking to find more suitable educational applications for 3D content. Indeed, there are already dedicated agencies targeting this area, such as Caper Interactive in the UK, which is developing a 3D environment in which children can learn the grammar and structure of foreign languages.

This is another area that Viewpoint is active in, as demonstrated in April 2001 when the company signed a strategic partnership with e-learning firm Edulink. The idea was to develop educational and distance-learning programs using Viewpoint's 3D technology, with the first project being an interactive 3D science lab. 'Science is best learned in a hands-on environment', said Edulink CEO, Michael Rosenfeld, at the time of the deal. 'We see the Viewpoint Experience Technology as a key element in making that setting an engaging and inviting format for a wider range of students and education providers.'

The corporate training side is equally interesting, with huge firms like Cisco already catching onto the potential of web 3D to show engineers and technical staff how different bits of equipment work. Cisco's Internet Learning Solutions Group (ILSG) started developing Shockwave 3D training content as soon as Macromedia launched Director 8.5, providing engineers with 3D visualizations of hardware and software products. In the future, staff will be able to access this kind of content on their PDA handheld devices, making it relevant to any profession where technical staff are out in the field installing hardware or fixing faults.

ANIMATION

To see how 3D animation might develop online, you just have to look at the movies. Hollywood went from 2D cartoons to full 3D computer-generated (CG) animation, and the web looks set to see the same transition. Until recently, designers have been restricted to Flash if they wanted to create non-linear animation, thus making it usually a 2D affair. Now, tools like Swift 3D mean that they can create 3D Flash animation. Also, there are export tools for all the high-end 3D modelling applications such as Maya, 3ds Max, Lightwave and Softimage — the tools that are used to create big-budget movies like Monsters Inc. and Shrek. It is now simple to output work created in these packages into a format that is suitable for viewing over the internet.

With this in mind, I expect to see the big Hollywood CG studios like Pixar making use of this, providing dedicated web trailers for their movies. What's more, the web will continue to offer independent 3D animators a distribution platform for their work. The major offline studios will be able to use the web as a source of ideas and talent, while the individual animators will be able to get their ideas to a wider audience. Hopefully, they will also investigate the web's potential

to add interactivity to 3D animation —
an area which we've only just started
to explore.

SPORTS

Another potential area for web 3D
is in the field of sports webcasting.
As broadband continues to roll out,
consumers will be hoping to watch
video highlights of their favourite
sports via their PC or mobile phones.
One of the selling points of the
upcoming third-generation (3G) mobile
phones is their mooted ability to
stream goal highlights, for example.
The problem lies in the question of
rights — thus far, governing bodies,
broadcasters and other interested
parties have only caused confusion by
trying to work out how this kind of
content will work.

Web 3D could offer a stopgap solution.
The technology is available to take
video footage of, say, a football
match, and turn it into a real-time 3D
animation. Web users can then watch the
'matches', choosing from an infinite
variety of camera angles — many of
which would be impossible in the real
world, for example, watching from the
referee's viewpoint, or floating just
behind the head of the striker.

The Israeli firm Orad formed a
dedicated subsidiary, OradNet, to
provide this service to broadcasters
who wished to show virtual highlights
online. It's still possible to see a
couple of sites that took them up on
the offer, and watch goal highlights

from the Spanish league. However,
the company is no longer operating in
this area. Nevertheless, it provides
a possibility for the future, for
another ambitious company to continue
their work.

NAVIGATION

So far, I've covered dedicated 3D
content, but it is also important
to consider the use of 3D interfaces
to present other kinds of web content.
Digit's MTV2 site seemed to herald
a new age of ambitious user-interface
design that could use 3D at the same
time as pleasing usability specialists
like Jakob Nielsen. As yet, however,
that hasn't happened.

The majority of corporate and ecommerce
sites have stuck to their traditional
top/left menu bar interfaces, while
even the more experimental sites have
tended to play it safe with 2D Flash
interfaces. Experiments like Virtual
Themeworld are intriguing, although it
remains to be seen how many corporate
clients will be willing to pay for
this kind of work.

The vast majority of the web's content
is still words and pictures, so truly
immersive 3D interfaces aren't going
to take off beyond the simple spatial
scheme of sites like MTV2. The
arguments are the same as those for
virtual supermarkets: there's little
point in creating an interface that
obstructs users from accessing the
content they want. Until some brave
web designers prove me wrong, I think

web 3D will be a content thing, rather than an interface thing.

Naturally, not everyone agrees. During the research for this book, I emailed Professor Ben Schneiderman, a US-based academic who gave the keynote speech at this year's Web 3D Conference. He pointed me in the direction of Win3D, a 3D interface for the Windows operating system that allows you to walk around 'rooms' to launch different applications and navigate through files. His implication was that this could foreshadow another possible future direction for web content.

Win3D is slick and technically impressive. It's fun to wander through a 3D representation of your file system. But there have been attempts in the past to create this kind of interface, and they didn't succeed. Win3D is certainly accomplished, but it isn't enough to tempt me away from my traditional 2D desktop. This is the problem facing any web designer looking to impose 3D interfaces onto content that remains stubbornly 2D. Nevertheless, I'm sure this won't stop some designers from trying — nor should it.

MOBILE DEVICES
When attempting to come to an overall conclusion about the future of web 3D, it's important to think about how 3D content will be delivered to users. It won't just be through their PCs — they'll also be able to access it through interactive TV, mobile phones

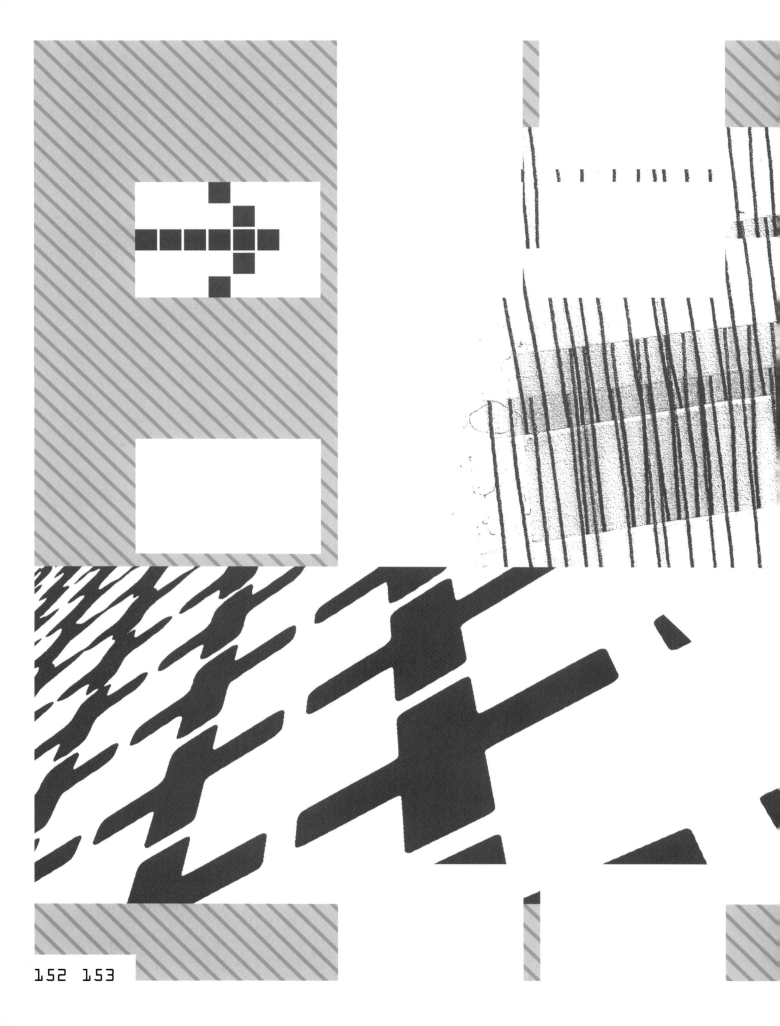

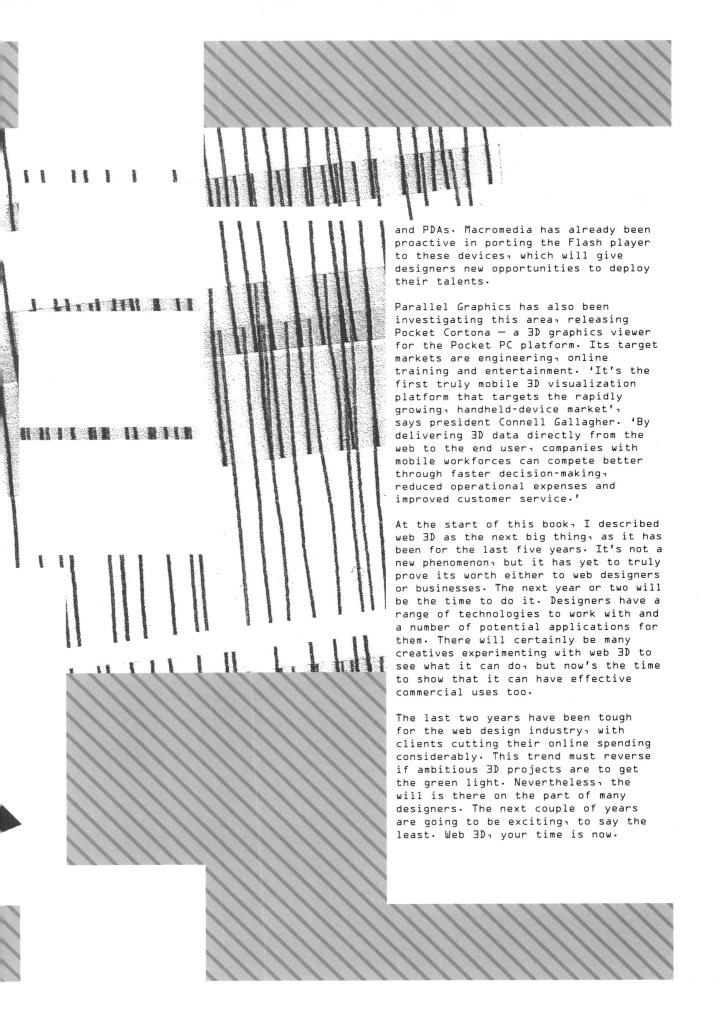

and PDAs. Macromedia has already been proactive in porting the Flash player to these devices, which will give designers new opportunities to deploy their talents.

Parallel Graphics has also been investigating this area, releasing Pocket Cortona — a 3D graphics viewer for the Pocket PC platform. Its target markets are engineering, online training and entertainment. 'It's the first truly mobile 3D visualization platform that targets the rapidly growing, handheld-device market', says president Connell Gallagher. 'By delivering 3D data directly from the web to the end user, companies with mobile workforces can compete better through faster decision-making, reduced operational expenses and improved customer service.'

At the start of this book, I described web 3D as the next big thing, as it has been for the last five years. It's not a new phenomenon, but it has yet to truly prove its worth either to web designers or businesses. The next year or two will be the time to do it. Designers have a range of technologies to work with and a number of potential applications for them. There will certainly be many creatives experimenting with web 3D to see what it can do, but now's the time to show that it can have effective commercial uses too.

The last two years have been tough for the web design industry, with clients cutting their online spending considerably. This trend must reverse if ambitious 3D projects are to get the green light. Nevertheless, the will is there on the part of many designers. The next couple of years are going to be exciting, to say the least. Web 3D, your time is now.

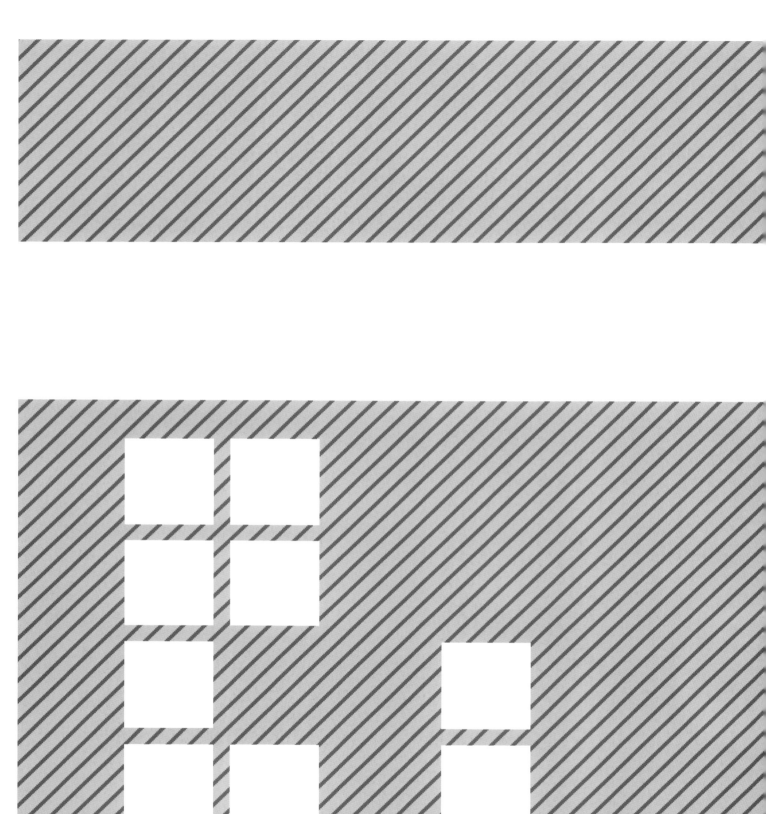

http//

RESOURCES

www.macromedia.com
Extremely slick and comprehensive site,
providing full support for Flash and
Director users, as well as dedicated video
tutorials for 3D Shockwave development.
Also includes Macromedia's Site Of The Day
section, which periodically features a new
3D site.

www.adobe.com/products/atmosphere/
The official home of Adobe Atmosphere.
Here you'll find the latest beta releases
of the development software and browser,
as well as tutorials, sample worlds and
forums to discuss the ins and outs of
the software.

www.viewpoint.com
The official site of one of the key
3D visualization players. Its Developer
Central section has a wealth of resources
for designers, including demos, tutorials,
forums, free software and a bi-weekly
developer newsletter.

www.aliaswavefront.com/en/Community/
Special/shockwave/shockwave_m.html
The home of the Maya Shockwave 3D
Exporter, a tool which enables high-end
3D modellers to export their work into
Shockwave for the web. As well as getting
your hands on the tool itself, here you'll
find technical info, demos and official
support.

www.parallelgraphics.com
One of the kingpins of the VRML world
is adapting well to the current state
of web 3D, continuing to innovate. This
site's Showroom section has a bunch of
impressive demos, while its Developer Zone
contains FAQs and resources for all the
company's products.

www.discreet.com/products/plasma/
Discreet is a relatively recent entrant
into the web 3D market, but if you're
intrigued by the firm's Plasma product,
this site should go some way to answering
your questions. And it's got a fine 3D
interface too.

www.cult3d.com
Cult3D is a popular web 3D tool,
created by a company called Cycore
(www.cycore.com). This dedicated site
features news of the latest sites using
the tool, as well as galleries, downloads
and tutorials.

www.swift3d.com
This product from Electric Rain enables
Flash designers to harness the power
of 3D in Macromedia's tool. This site
provides downloads as a standalone tool,
as well as plug-ins for 3D animation
tools 3ds Max, Softimage and Lightwave.

www.web3d.org
This is the Web3D Consortium, which
has been heavily involved in online
development since the days of VRML.
Now, this is the essential destination
if you want to find out about the new X3D
standard, which is rising to prominence.

www.sho.com/alt/expo/labzone/
Excellent site showcasing the latest
developments in web 3D, from animations
through to games. It's a magazine format,
with interviews with key figures in the
web 3D development community, as well as
articles on innovative sites. Well worth
a look.

www.directoru.com/community/3D/
The Director University's 3D section,
which provides much to chew on if you're
working on 3D Shockwave content. It's run
by some of the world's most experienced
Director users, making it an authoritative
source for information and technical help.

www.atmoinfopool.com
Bilingual German and English site run by
designer Maik Ludewig — see Spacelounge
case study — as a resource for Atmosphere
developers. It features tutorials, tips,
sample avatars and galleries of worlds
to explore.

www.atmospherians.com
Extremely well-stocked Atmosphere
developer site. One of the best outlets
for news of new worlds, as well as the
usual news, sample avatars and community
discussion. The Atmosphere development
community is thriving — this site is one
of the reasons why.

www.3dlinks.com
Although this site covers all 3D
development, including offline animation
and modelling, it still offers useful
links for web 3D developers, particularly
those using Shockwave or Poser.

www.macweb3d.org
Although web 3D is often seen as a
PC-based thing, there is a healthy
community of Mac-based developers working
on innovative projects. This is one of
the more popular sites serving this group
of designers.

www.3dfestival.com
One of the more popular 3D festivals,
which includes coverage of web 3D
content. It's periodically updated in
between events, but it is worth checking
out to find the date and location of the
next one.

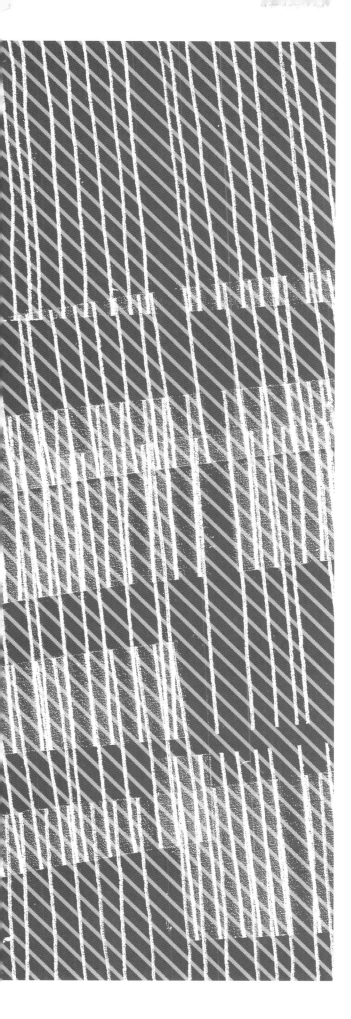

"Web 3D is going to be a major
element in the years to come: from
product display and exciting chat
environments to the selling of homes
and teamgaming. The possibilities
merely need to be tapped."
George Lippert, web 3D designer

the end